1981

autoBiographical

Look at

Carol Roger
&
the Client centered

approach)

Counseling
Theories
and
Techniques

Lester N. Downing

Counseling
Theories
and
Techniques:

Summarized and Critiqued
(A Competency-Based Approach)

nh Nelson-Hall
Chicago

Library of Congress Cataloging in Publication Data

Downing, Lester N.
  Counseling theories and techniques.

  Bibliography: p.
  Includes index.
  1. Counseling. 2. Psychotherapy. I. Title.
BF637.C6D62   158   74-23725
ISBN: 0–88229–203–X (cloth)
ISBN: 0–88229–502–O (paper)

Downing Lester N.
counseling theories
& techniques.
Nelson Hall
Chicago. copyright
1975-77 pp. 59, 60, 61
& 71

Contents

Features of growth counseling
Summary

Preface

This text deals with the major theories of counseling and psychotherapy. Its uniqueness lies in its simplified summary of important theories and in its meaningful critique of each theory. The "systems approach" covering each chapter is an innovation for this type of textbook, and it permits an objective evaluation of each student's progress in the course.

The text allows for and encourages the use of other references, while still providing the essential framework of study within the one text. It makes possible an intensive study of counseling theory in a minimum of time. The research needed to provide information contained in the text has been done by the author. The student's efforts may thus be centered upon gaining a deep understanding of each theory, and in developing the skills of each theory without a great commitment of time and energy.

This text should prove to be very popular with professors and students in appropriate psychology and counselor education courses that are designed to prepare people as counselors and psychotherapists.

These will include upper division undergraduates, but more particularly graduate students, in colleges and universities. Other personnel in the helping and education professions, mental health clinics, public schools, and community agencies should find this book to be useful and its approach exciting.

This text has the following main purposes: (1) to meet the need of students for a readable, succinct summary of the main counseling theories; (2) to provide a framework and a beginning point for a more intensive study of counseling, made available in other texts; (3) to further clarify the similarities and differences between and among the various counseling theories; (4) to introduce the growth counseling concept; (5) to identify some of the limitations of the various theories and approaches; and to show how growth counseling attempts to minimize these limitations; (6) to provide a systems approach model for the study of theories through the use of performance objectives; (7) to show the reader an approach to the study of counseling that may be informative and exciting; (8) to provide a framework for the study of counseling that may be profitably utilized far into the future; (9) to show the relationship between theory and practice and to help the student gain a full realization as to need and place of both in effective counseling; and (10) to demonstrate the excitement to be found in a study of counseling theory and techniques, and in the satisfactions gained from seeing people change their behavior and find greater satisfaction in living.

I acknowledge the motivating influence of students and colleagues in the demanding task of writing this text. Their perceptions, observations, and expectations made the need for care and accuracy in summarizing the theories a rather sensitive one. However, I make no claim to perfection in my interpretations of these theories. This attitude thus encourages the reader to freely express himself on any flaws he may detect. I do assume full responsibility for my statements about growth counseling. I find it easier to say what I believe than to try to say what someone else believes. While I can feel as well as intellectualize my beliefs, I can only intellectualize in a kind of second-hand fashion the beliefs of others.

I acknowledge the astute observations of Dr. Dan Wynkoop in making the reports on some of the theories more authentic. The encouragement of Dr. Curtis Van Alfen, dean of the college of education, for productive and innovative action by faculty members is gratefully acknowledged.

/ 1 /

An introduction to the counseling process

Counseling has always meant something a little different to each individual who has concerned himself with this activity. To the layman, counseling has meant essentially advising, telling, and directing. He has regarded these as the main functions of the counselor in helping a person resolve his problems, improve his behavior, and make appropriate plans for the future. Such advice and direction from the counselor presumably result in fewer mistakes and better adjustments by the individual seeking assistance.

Unfortunately, the views and understandings of some educators have been similar to those of the layman as to the true purpose and meaning of counseling. However, the increasing opportunities of the past decade for educators to become better informed on many subjects, including counseling, have resulted in a new conceptualization of counseling. It is now seen as an in-depth, personal experience with many possibilities for the individual to gain insights and understanding about himself and others. It is also seen as a prelude to significant and meaningful behavior changes, and to appropriate decision making.

Counseling is now viewed as a dynamic, intimate personal relationship between counselor and client, marked by a high degree of meaningful involvement and interaction. The specific techniques used are outcomes of, as well as preludes to, the kind of a relationship developed within the counseling setting. A particular technique may be utilized by the counselor as the nature of the problem and the relationship suggests. Techniques are also readily abandoned or more fully utilized as the judgment of the counselor and the unique needs of the client dictate.

With the changes in philosophy and techniques in counseling, in response to the demands of a changing world, we might assume an abandonment of the theoretical orientations of the past. In reality just the reverse is the case. The need has never been greater for a fuller and more comprehensive utilization of all concepts and approaches that hold promise for assisting people today.

A successful utilization of past and current knowledge in counseling depends, then, upon a careful selection of those ideas, concepts, facts, philosophies, and principles with the best possibilities for practical application in meeting current problems. To do this, we must first know what each counseling theory or approach has to offer. We must then be sufficiently familiar with today's world and its citizens to know how to best proceed in order to provide the needed help for each individual who seeks assistance from a counselor.

Major themes of this text

A textbook is more than an accumulation of information, as it also provides for a source of organized data and ideas for the reader. The material presented must, therefore, be meaningful, and it must make sense to him. He need not agree with all of the ideas presented, but he should know what these ideas are and the promise they hold for him. He should, in other words, be able to profit from his experience with the book. The stimulation he receives from his study should then result in an increase in the depth and scope of his own thought processes and in the quality and intensity of his action.

The theme of a textbook is the heart of what the author is trying to convey to the reader. It is the essence of his message and point of view. It is from the theme that the reader receives his direction for profound thought and forceful action. The information gained from the reading serves to augment the central theme.

The theme of this text is divided into six main elements, each of which is discussed below.

Importance of theory

All the theories of counseling and psychotherapy have something to offer the counselor. Each theory is the product of many years of intensive thought, meaningful experience, and relevant research by competent and dedicated individuals. The concepts developed, conclusions reached, and ideas expressed inevitably provide important information and direction for the counselor. He is a better informed and more imaginative counselor by virtue of his encounter with ideas in this book. The degree to which he agrees or disagrees with the ideas expressed is relatively unimportant. What is important is that he receive some stimulation and direction toward the formulation of his own ideas and the improvement of his skills.

All theories that are currently acceptable to and identified by counseling and psychotherapy have something to offer the counselor. This includes the traditional psychoanalytic theory of Sigmund Freud as well as the more recent theories of the rational-emotive therapy developed by Albert Ellis and the reality therapy of William Glasser. Each theory has made, and is continuing to make, its unique contribution to counseling and psychotherapy.

Other theories and approaches will continue to appear on the scene and to have an impact upon current thought. An example of these is transactional analysis. This is seen by many of us as an exciting and promising counseling method, and more importantly, as a structure for meaningful living. The limited scope of this text does not permit more than a brief reference to transactional analysis, but it is seen as a bright light within the field of counseling and psychotherapy.

Essentiality of a theoretical framework

Theory provides ideas and guidelines for the counselor, and it constitutes a framework of operation upon which the counselor can depend for direction in his counseling. It is within the framework that he selects and utilizes the most promising techniques for effective counseling.

Theory also provides a philosophical orientation from which the counselor may draw in assessing and solidifying his own philosophical position on points critical to man's welfare. The approach of the counselor is determined in a large sense by his beliefs as to the nature, conditions, and fate of mankind. No one person has the wisdom or the intelligence to arrive at conclusive answers to tremendously profound and challenging questions. He needs to draw from the thinking of others from both the past and the present. Unanswered questions will no doubt continue to plague civilization, but the lack of answers need not deter growth and progress.

Assessment of theory

The constant assessment of theory is basic to a counselor's increasing competence and effectiveness. He need not accept or reject all elements of any one theory. Essentially, his task is to utilize the elements of one or more theories in accordance with his best judgment.

Assessment thus results in the use of those elements that are in closest harmony with the counselor's current views, and it is most helpful in applying the techniques with which he is most familiar. Assessment is also applied to the counselor's ideas and methods for purposes of improving them as he learns from his study and experience.

Development of new concepts

New theories emerge from the conceptualization of ideas gained from probing and challenging existing theory and from the stimulation gleaned from broad experiences. The development of new concepts, then, constitutes the fourth element within the theme of this book. The material presented in the discussions here includes brief summaries of the major counseling theories and a critique of each theory. This format provides an example of how every counselor may approach a study of theory.

Generally, the steps are as follows: (1) each theory is carefully studied and the main ideas are identified; (2) a summary is made of the major points in the theory; (3) each point is judiciously critiqued; and (4) statements are then made denoting the position of the author on each summarized element of the theory.

The next possibility open to the individual is to go a step beyond the above and propose some ideas that are either extensions of an existing idea or completely new. New concepts may thus emerge and constitute forerunners to possible new theories.

Relationship of counseling to personality

In this fifth part of the theme, we emphasize that all counseling must consider and have a close relationship to the individual. A particular technique is effective to the degree to which it is acceptable to and compatible with the personality of the individual being counseled. The counselor must, therefore, be well informed on theory and be imaginative in the application of concepts gained from theory.

The counselor must then utilize the counseling relationship as a source of stimulation and direction for the client. It is the client who must find within this relationship those elements that prompt him toward improved behavior and better adjustment. This will happen only if the counselor is sufficiently resourceful and insightful to make the counseling approach appropriately harmonious with the uniqueness of the individual client.

Counseling techniques and personal growth

The value of a particular approach lies in those elements that promote the growth of the individual. If his potentialities for growth are probed and his energies are properly triggered, then the outcomes of counseling should be positive. Problem resolution remains as only one objective of counseling; the major goal is permanent and continuous growth characterized by a vital interest in life and a profound concern for what constitutes meaningful living.

Meaning and nature of counseling and psychotherapy

We frequently bemoan the lack of theory to cover a certain aspect of education, such as guidance (Sprinthall 1971). We also feel a need for additional theory for counseling. Perhaps this is due to dissatisfaction with currently available theories, accompanied by the hope that something better will soon emerge. Theories do indeed exist, but how well they satisfy the counselor is another matter.

We feel, then, that a basic knowledge of theory is essential to a comprehensive understanding of counseling, and to an understanding of self. It is from this philosophical base that the counselor is able to bring his talents and expertise to bear in helping the client. Such knowledge is also helpful to the counselor in his own growth-promoting efforts. Only as his own self-understanding deepens and broadens will he reach a level of maximum effectiveness in assisting others. Our description of counseling in this text continually emphasizes the importance of theory as a guide in all counseling and psychotherapy.

Although the terms "counseling" and "psychotherapy" are used interchangeably for the purpose of simplicity, there are some practical differences. "Counseling" is generally used to designate the work of the counselor in an educational setting with individuals whose problems are not deep-seated or disabling. "Psychotherapy" typically describes the work of the psychotherapist in a medical or clinical setting with individuals experiencing relatively severe emotional problems. The competence and qualifications of the persons performing these services are also distinguishing factors. The psychotherapist is medically and clinically trained, while the counselor's preparation is essentially educational.

Counseling defined

Basic to all counseling is the belief that it must provide the stimulation and the direction essential to continuous emotional and intellectual growth by the client. The resolution of an immediate problem is only one facet of counseling. It must also be a source of possibilities for growth, which is characterized by increasing insights and understanding, better utilization of intellectual and emotional resources, and continuous and meaningful changes in behavior. Theory is heavily utilized in achieving these objectives.

Counseling is a process and an activity engaged in by a qualified counselor and an individual seeking assistance. Its purposes include aiding the person in resolving his problem, making plans, reducing conflicts, achieving better adjustment, and effecting needed behavior changes. The precise techniques of the counselor in achieving these goals depend upon his skill and orientation and the particular needs, characteristics, and expectations of the client.

Normally, counseling is limited to one counselor and one client, unless the approach used is group counseling in which several clients are accommodated by one, and sometimes two, counselors. The principles and concepts of group counseling are essentially the same as those in individual counseling, so the major difference is in the number of participants. The quality of the relationship receives greater stress in some theories than in others, however.

Psychotherapy defined

Psychotherapy is a process by which a qualified psychotherapist helps an individual seeking assistance make substantial changes in his personality structure for purposes of more effective functioning. The treatment is generally of long duration and quite intensive, and it involves diagnostic procedures. These procedures include the identification of the causes of the difficulty and the prescription of courses of action. The overcoming of emotional problems and conflicts receives the immediate and direct attention of the psychotherapist.

As in counseling, the precise techniques of the therapist depend upon a number of conditions. These include the therapist's skill with a particular approach, his philosophy and orientation, the receptivity, stability, and maturity of the patient, and the availability of treatment tools and facilities. Variety and breadth characterize the many approaches used in both counseling and psychotherapy.

Psychotherapy is the clinical service through which individuals suffering from emotional problems may gain some relief. Frequently, the individual beset with conflicts and other difficulties is unable to see his way out of his problems. A therapist may help the patient by explaining to him the possible causes of his difficulties and by prescribing appropriate treatment. Most individuals perform more effectively if they are able to overcome the energy-usurping problems that inevitably block their progress. A competent therapist is frequently able to provide the treatment needed to help the individual overcome his problems and increase his effectiveness.

Significant developments in counseling

A number of very significant developments have occurred and are continuing to occur in counseling. The events and crises of the world and society continue to contribute to the long list of implications that these events create for the counselor. Urbanization, poverty, drugs, pollution, population control, morality, and many other conditions are sources of frighteningly formidable problems. Although it is not within the scope of this publication to do more than mention these problems, we are concerned about the implications these conditions have for the counseling profession. It is the intent to identify some developments in counseling, some of which have a direct relationship to the critical problems of the world.

New attitudes toward the individual

The concern for following a particular approach or set of techniques in counseling has given way to a more intensive consideration for the personal welfare of the individual. Counseling techniques are thus undergoing rapid and dramatic changes. There is a new and vigorous attempt to develop a kind of relationship in counseling from which the individual gains renewed hope as the relationship attempts to provide for his unique needs.

Each person is viewed by the counselor as a dynamically and potentially effective individual, and his possibilities for progress, growth, and achievements are viewed as legion. The individual's major limitations are frequently seen by the counselor as self-imposed. The person himself is often his most serious deterrent to growth. The main problem of the counselor is to get the individual to see himself realistically and optimistically and to utilize himself and his resources for obtaining the desired objectives.

High self-confidence and a positive self-esteem are seen by the counselor as essential prerequisites to an effective and productive performance by the individual. These are characteristics that can be developed within the person. They are no longer left to chance for their development, nor is their possession regarded as an act of fate.

Creativity is likewise viewed by the counselor as a most desirable trait, the initiation and development of which may be accomplished through a stimulating environment. Counseling is an indispensable part of that environment with inherent possibilities for prodding and encouraging the individual toward highly productive action.

The professionalization of counseling

Considerable effort has gone into making counseling a recognized profession by the American Personnel and Guidance Association and two of its divisions: the American School Counselors Association and the Association for Counselor Education and Supervision. Essential to the professionalization of counseling has been the establishment of guidelines and the general upgrading of preparation. The counselor's role and his functions have also been the focus of attention. A much clearer understanding now exists as to the true role of the counselor in education and as to the precise functions he is to perform.

Codes of ethics have also been developed by professional organizations within the American Personnel and Guidance Associations. Such codes have resulted in a keener awareness by training institutions as to their responsibilities in properly preparing individuals for counseling positions. These codes are also useful to practicing counselors as instruments for self-assessment and personal evaluation.

The emergence of the concept supporting the need for counselors in the elementary school, as well as the secondary school, has occurred. Counselors at all educational levels are thus seen as members of a new and unique profession.

The changing role of the counselor

Traditionally, the counselor's role has been perceived essentially as that of a helper and an advisor. His job was to assist students with course and program selections and to listen attentively and sympathetically to their problems and concerns. The life of the counselor is no longer this simple. His role is much broader as he involves himself in a very personal way in the total development of the individual.

A rapidly changing and anxiety-evoking world is producing a very different young citizen from his counterpart of previous generations. His needs are different and his demands are more intense. The role of the counselor must likewise change in response to these new expectations. He must be able to help young people probe, explore, evaluate, and develop their own internal resources. He must help them see that the answers to many of their problems and to the attainment of emotional stability, in an otherwise shaky environment, rest with themselves. This kind of direction and encouragement requires far more assistance from the counselor than the conventional advisor's role.

The counselor should be a well-adjusted, resourceful, imaginative, optimistic, and creative person. The persuasion and positive influence of the counselor thus comes through to the client, resulting in hopeful insights in which he sees the growth possibilities open to him. The counselor should also be able to make needed adaptations and adjustments in order to fully accommodate each client. His ability to sense a person's needs and concerns and his skill in working effectively with that person within the limits of his intellectual and emotional perceptions are also essential. The counselor must also have the sensitivity to perceive any possible misunderstandings harbored by the client about the counseling relationship, and he must have the ability to clarify these. Mutual respect, warmth, understanding, and a cooperative attitude should characterize the relationship. Any tendency toward disillusionment, suspicion, or disappointment should be eliminated. The counselor's effectiveness, as well as the client's progress, depend upon a quality relationship that provides the client with the stimulation, encouragement, and direction upon which his continuing progress and success depend.

The emergence of the concept that stresses the counselor's role as a consultant (Fullmer and Bernard 1972) lends variety to the changing role of the counselor. As these authors suggest, this approach is not new, it is just a matter of getting various parts of the school system to work together in a coordinated manner. Frequently, the counselor has not functioned as an effective member of the educational team. This weakness must, obviously, be corrected. Evidence suggests that improvements are being made as more intensive efforts are being given to involving the counselor in the total educational enterprise. Counselor and teacher roles are changing to better accommodate and utilize their individual skills and talents.

Adapting counseling to student needs

As more attention is paid to the psychology of development and to the unique needs of each student, greater efforts are being made to change counseling philosophies and approaches. The attitude is one of suggesting that there is no finality in any one approach or theory and that theories and techniques are the servants of the counselor, not his master.

The counselor should obviously be well informed on the major counseling theories. It is from this background of academic knowledge that he is able to accommodate the client through appropriate techniques and procedures.

The counselor should adopt and maintain an attitude of flexibility concerning himself and should be able to reduce or eliminate any tendency toward rigidity or conventionalism. The fact that the counselor's orientations, beliefs, and experiences may be quite different from his clients' should in no way interfere with his ability to work effectively with the client.

The changing emphasis on different counseling approaches

Historically, the psychoanalytic approach has dominated the psychotherapeutic scene. Even counselors functioning without medical or clinical training were influenced by Freudian theory. However, developments in counseling and psychotherapy include some startling departures from the traditional psychoanalytic viewpoints. These departures have resulted in the emergence of some therapeutic approaches that have capitalized upon the lessons learned from the Freudians, while still pressing for more meaningful ways to help people. The challenges of the times and the renewed emphasis upon the importance of the individual have contributed to thought and action in initiating new approaches.

These new approaches are characterized by rationality, logic, reality, and intellectualization. The intent is to help the individual to see himself and his environment realistically and to act in a manner consistent with his own best good. The environment, including societal expectations and demands, is to be utilized appropriately and realistically, because to oppose the inevitable is to create a situation incompatible with one's best interests and achievements.

Expedient changes in behavior are promoted in most of these new or modified therapies. The purpose of therapy is to encourage the individual to abandon unproductive and debilitating behaviors and adopt behaviors holding greater promise for the fulfillment of needs. This assumes an ability to unlearn as well as to learn certain behaviors.

The need for changes in counseling

Some reference has been made in this chapter to those conditions that contribute to a need for counseling and for changes in counseling approaches. This section focuses more precisely upon those conditions that dictate a need for meaningful counseling in the lives of people.

A radically changing society

Conditions within the world are changing at an unprecedented rate, and the impact of these changes is having a tremendous influence upon all citizens. The ability of the individual to anticipate and adapt to change and his skill in utilizing change to his own advantage significantly determine his status in society. His emotional well-being also depends upon his flexibility, adaptability, and resourcefulness.

Some of these changes with perhaps the greatest implications for counseling include the following.

1. The economy. A changing economic structure, which permits and encourages indebtedness and fosters an attitude of affluence, continues to create problems for many people. The desire to savor life's many joys has contributed to a condition of fiscal irresponsibility.

2. Morality. The reduction or elimination of barriers to acts once regarded as immoral has resulted in an attitude of permissiveness and acceptance. As prohibitions and censures are reduced, individuals are faced with decisions of the greatest magnitude. Credulity and acceptance have become a way of life. Certainly the need for help in decision making and in the establishment of appropriate values has never been greater. The temptations of the times are overwhelming, and the intrigues and fascinations of promised excitement continue to lure the unwary.

3. Freedom. A new sense of freedom, which exceeds the limits of freedom in its conventional sense, pervades society. There appears to be, in the minds of many, a forceful anticipation of some glorious wonderland marked only by joys and thrills. Responsibility no longer holds as firm a place in the minds of many people as has been true in the past. A redefinition of terms, such as freedom, is very much in evidence.

4. Involvements. Stimulating involvements of the individual with other people underlie a recognition for the need to change. The relevance of close, warm relationships with other humans to one's own development is now recognized. Greater freedoms contribute to this condition as they foster more meaningful relationships among individuals. The lessening of restrictive inhibitions is contributing to an extension of the individual's circle of friends and associates. There is now a relatively loose, free-wheeling attitude that permits considerable latitude in thought and actions.

5. *Pollution.* A contamination of the environment at a frightening rate and the creation of irreversible blight and destruction in virtually all areas of the world have created some undeniably formidable problems. The casual acceptance of seemingly inevitable and ruinous havoc upon the land has long since become intolerable. The pollution of the intellect and of the emotions through pornography, and other evidences of liberality, is likewise taking its toll in human deterioration. A capitulation by the populace to these conditions could lead to permanent ruination. Forces mustered for a defense against destruction need to be encouraged and bolstered.

6. *Population explosion.* The world may be overcrowded, or becoming so, or there may be great inefficiency in the management of the world's affairs, thus giving the impression that the fault rests with overpopulation. In any case, the fight for survival and for the better life requires the full utilization of intelligence and the development of new managerial skills from which improvements can be realized.

7. *Poverty.* Unfulfilled needs for the basic life requirements continue to haunt the lives of many disadvantaged families and individuals. Society, with all its changes and declared advancements, has experienced only mediocre success in learning how to best accommodate its citizens at the lower economic levels.

8. *Urbanization.* Shifts in the urban population, and a change in the nature of that population, have brought into focus some new kinds of problems. The inner city has become the center of strife as the problems have outdistanced the solutions.

Changes in occupational structure

Advancing technology is beginning to dictate the course for many occupations and professions. The relative simplicity of choosing and of pursuing a life's work a thing of the past. Complexity characterizes many of the developing occupations, requiring, in some cases, skills for which little or no training is available. The demands in some occupations upon the intellect and resourcefulness of the individual are alarmingly real. Selectivity is becoming a major factor in job training and placement.

Mediocrity in aptitude and performance is likely to be rewarded with unemployment or a dreary job. The expectation for the worker to be an economic asset to his employer is felt throughout all business and industry. Any tendency toward humaneness and patience by employers toward workers is rapidly nullified by the necessity of business to meet existing competition.

The influence of labor organizations continues to result in improvements in working conditions and wages for workers. However, it is the quality of the economic structure that ultimately determines the financial welfare of the individual. Jobs and occupations suitable to the individual must exist, and the individual must, in turn, be prepared with the necessary skills and productive capability to make his job tenable and permanent.

Changes in family structure

Theoretically, the family is the core and the hub of society. Practically, however, in view of mobility possibilities, new freedoms, and greater affluence, the family structure is undergoing change. The roles of family members are becoming more fluid, and a sense of increasing independence is occurring among children. The typical family, therefore, has relatively less influence upon the attitudes and behaviors of its members, but at the same time finds itself with burdensome financial demands. Each child in the family becomes aware at an early age of life's many attractions, and he quite readily assumes that his desires will be promptly met by indulgent parents. These conditions sometimes prompt stressful situations between the child and his parents and contribute to the frustrations of both.

The greater freedoms in family life result in more opportunities for the child to make decisions and engage in a variety of activities. As the family becomes less traditional and provides less protection against the world's affairs and events, the child must learn to assume more responsibility for himself. This may be devastating for the individual who lacks the necessary maturity, experience, and judgment to meet the complexity of challenges in a complicated world.

A new view of theory

Changes in the whole concept of counseling, and in the approaches to be used, are in order. These are based upon a more critical appraisal of·counseling theory. The relatively apathetic adherence to the dictates of a particular theory is rapidly losing favor. Many counselors have learned through hard and, in some cases, disappointing experiences that the conventional and prescribed approaches frequently fail to do the job. Clients too often are not helped by the counselor. He may listen attentively, warmly, and empathetically and even provide considerable support, but the individual continues to flounder and his problems flourish. The individual must be helped toward meaningful behavior changes, and he must become more effective in his endeavors, or the counseling was of questionable value. Abandonment of theory is obviously not the answer, but neither is a strict adherence to theory. The imaginative use of theory, combined with an extension of concepts and experimentation with newer approaches, are drastically needed for these times.

The kind of progress suggested here can be achieved by:
1. Identifying the main concepts in each of the current theories.
2. Making a critical analysis of each concept.
3. Selecting the concepts that appear to have a place in modern counseling theory.
4. Modifying the concepts as needed to fit a more progressive approach.
5. Adding those ideas needed to develop more helpful and realistic approaches.
6. Practicing the approaches suggested by this modified theoretical approach.

7. Researching and experimenting to constantly attain sound data from which to make additional modifications.

The employment of these procedures, and the development of a positive attitude toward substantial changes in theory and the approaches used, should result in some noteworthy improvements in counseling effectiveness.

Summary

The main themes of this text promote a logical use of current theories, while extending and developing some new or additional concepts. A broad definition of counseling and psychotherapy permits flexibility within concepts and in the application of these concepts.

New developments in counseling and psychotherapy encourage a more imaginative use of theory and more innovative approaches by the counselor in his work. The role of the counselor is changing in response to the need for innovation and for devising better ways of helping people resolve their problems.

The rapid and significant changes within society make the need for advancements in counseling and psychotherapy even more critical.

Study and discussion problems

1. Account for the misunderstandings concerning the true meaning of counseling.
2. Express in your own words what you feel is the theme of this text.
3. Define counseling and describe a situation in which counseling is used. This might be demonstrated.
4. Define psychotherapy and give an example showing how it is used.
5. The author outlines some developments in counseling. Point out some implications that each of these has for the counselor.
6. Identify some conditions in society that dictate the need for some substantial changes in counseling.

/ 2 /

A theoretical framework for counseling

All counseling approaches and techniques should have the benefit of some theoretical underpinnings upon which to depend. It is from this position and under this framework that the counselor may apply those techniques which seem most suitable for him and for his client. Since it is true that no one school of counseling is adequate (Berenson and Carkhuff 1967), the counselor will likely be more effective as he draws information and ideas from several theories. In this case he is constantly in the process of developing an appropriate personal theory. His own scholarship should continue to improve as he keeps abreast of trends in theory, and likewise, his skills should become better as he experiences reinforcement for his efforts.

Although the greatest part of a counselor's effectiveness can be accounted for independently of his theoretical orientation (Berenson and Carkhuff 1967), it would be erroneous to conclude that theory has no part to play in counseling effectiveness. The helping processes of empathy, positive regard, genuineness, and concreteness, which ultimately bring the greatest client gains, are really essential conditions in most theoretical approaches. Their effective use depends upon the counselor's familiarity with theory.

In this chapter we identify the main aspects of theory and note that there is probably no such thing as a practical approach without a foundation of theory. The main theoretical forces underlying current theory are reviewed. These include associationism, classical psychoanalysis, and humanistic psychology.

The practicality of theory

Lister's (1967) suggestion that there is nothing so practical as a good theory has merit in this discussion. It provides a basis for action and a rationale for practice, as it serves as a map for exploring unfamiliar terrain. The theory aversion that appears to characterize the attitudes of many counselors should be a matter of considerable concern to us. This attitude may account, at least in part, for the confusion demonstrated by some counselors and for the relative ineffectiveness of those same counselors. Theory aversion has also been found to be a deterrent to the development of guidance programs in schools (Peters 1963). The implications for counselor training programs are quite clear. It may be easier and more satisfying initially to concentrate on techniques and ignore theory in training, but this could be a shortcut to mediocrity for the counselor. It is not my intent to bend the prospective counselor to fit a particular theory but rather to capitalize upon theory for purposes of helping him realize professional and personal growth. The growth to which I refer underlies a continuous and increasing competence of the counselor.

The status of theory

A study of theory and its application in counseling practice serves the counselor as a means to worthy ends, which includes greater counseling skill. The counselor does not become a slave to theory, but rather its master, as he utilizes the concepts found in the various theories to his own and the client's advantage. He profits from a knowledge of the concepts found in theory as he is prompted to explore ideas from which he can develop better counseling approaches. The relationship between counselor and client is strengthened, not because of adherence to theory, but rather by virtue of the counselor's greater scholarship and skill. Counselor education programs must, then, have a strong commitment to a study of theory, with the assumption that the knowledge and understanding gained will be instrumental in bringing the counselor to a high level of competence.

As we learn to use theory to our best advantage, we will note the inevitable overlap of concepts among the different theories. Rare is the concept that is the exclusive property of just one theory. It is more a matter of degree of emphasis or importance given to an element by a particular theory. The counselor should be sensitive to this element in a particular theory. The counselor should be sensitive to this condition and then avoid any tendency to give full credit for an idea to just one theory. The various theories continue to borrow from each other and at the same time share their contributions. Chenault's (1968, p. 111) "syntony" has merit as a perception of life, rejecting the either-or meanings of events, experiences, feelings, or concepts. We might find it advantageous to think of many of the identified elements in theories as really being sufficiently broad to find a haven in more than one theory. As Chenault suggests, ". . . theory's purpose need not always necessarily be to lead to the prediction and control of behavior" (p. 112).

The meaning of theory

There are many definitions of a theory (Stefflre 1965; Patterson 1966). A theory has meaning for the individual, and it contributes to the effectiveness of his work as it synthesizes data and makes them more manageable. Each has value as it helps in the clarification of thinking and in the establishment of sound procedures.

A theory may be viewed, then, as a "platform from which to view phenomena and a system for unifying within a professional self the meaning of a learning" (Bower and Hollister 1967, p. viii). Its relevance to the learner is then determined by his knowledge and perceptions of the surrounding phenomena, resulting in theory having a personal meaning for the individual.

Our purposes in this text may be met by defining theory as an accumulation of carefully considered ideas that provide a framework for functioning and for the inception of new ideas. Theory has value as it provides a conceptual structure by which behavior is explained and as it provides guidelines for the modification of behavior. Theory also sets the course for the development of hypotheses, which, after being tested, permit the establishment of certain conclusions.

The need for theory

The fact that counseling for young children still lacks a firm foundation in theory and research (Aubrey 1967) makes the need for theory development even more critical. This condition is inevitable in view of the relative recency of concerted attention to this aspect of a child's education. The counseling theory most appropriate for application by school counselors with small children has not yet been determined (Dinkmeyer 1967), but some progress is currently being made to develop such theory. The availability of theories developed essentially for adults, and in some cases adolescents, has been much more satisfactory.

The lag in developing theories suitable for young children has been due in part to a tendency to make programs designed to serve the secondary school also serve the elementary school. The differences between secondary and elementary school pupils are sufficiently pronounced as to require some clear-cut differences in the programs (Aubrey 1967; Dinkmeyer 1965). However, the needs of children at the various age levels are sufficiently alike that current theories may be used in developing more suitable theories for younger children. Current theories may also be improved upon in order to better meet the needs of older children and of adults.

The implications for this condition include the need for innovative thinking and resourcefulness in theory development. Also needed is some clear thinking as to the true purposes of counseling. Their establishment is essential to theory development. Tentativeness will no doubt characterize these efforts, but such attempts will bring some fruitful results in terms of guidelines for effective counseling.

Main theoretical forces underlying current theory

A counseling theory emerges gradually as an outcome of considerable effort, exploration, experience, and research. Since ideas, notions, and hypotheses underlie all theories at some point, time and the talents of individuals are required. There is no assurance, however, that these efforts will ever result in the emergence and acceptance of a theory. Most ideas remain as such, and most hypotheses are never adequately tested; thus, any set of ideas that is eventually accepted by the profession as a theory has undergone a rather rigorous assessment.

Historically, we find that a few major theories have provided the framework for relatively new theories. The emergence of these theories came only after considerable time. Their true worth was then found in the influence they wielded in the development of new or related theories. We also find that the current theories utilized in counseling and psychotherapy also belong to other areas of psychology. Counseling has thus depended upon these theories and has adopted many of them for use in counseling.

Counseling has been concerned about the implications associated with the use of theory. Counselors have not enjoyed the same immunity to the ethical implications of a theory as have the individuals who developed the theory. The counselor must be able to apply in a practical way any element of a theory he chooses to accept. In other words, it has to be more than a theoretical statement. It must have application possibilities. The counselor is the practitioner who puts the theory to the ultimate test.

In this section we look at the three main theoretical forces in psychology that have had a major impact upon thought in counseling and psychotherapy. These are associationism, classical psychoanalysis (Freudianism), and humanistic psychology (Bruce 1966).

Associationism

Associationism has had a long and eventful history, and its influences have been most pronounced. Philosophers have described the mind as having a number of thoughts, ideas, and sensations, which though isolated, were bound together through appropriate associations. Animal research contributed to a knowledge of the stimulus-response formula, which has in turn had a great influence upon thinking. E. L. Thorndike and others explored learning as a series of stimulus-response connections. An idea or sensation was in reality a response to an earlier idea or sensation. Principles were then developed by which learning could be explained as the establishment of a bond between a stimulus and a response.

Obviously, this theory, along with its many modifications, has had an impact upon education and upon society. The work of B. F. Skinner with reinforcement and programmed learning reflects certain elements of associationism. The many implications coming from this theoretical framework have constituted real challenges to educators. Skinner's belief that some control of human behavior is desirable prompts some inevitable ethical questions. Who is to say what the behavior of an individual is to be? The school, including its counseling service, should be influential in helping a person decide upon and practice behavior most suitable to need fulfillment and most compatible with society's expectations.

Classical psychoanalysis

Classical psychoanalysis has been a potent force among clinical psychologists, psychotherapists, and counselors (Bruce 1966). Sigmund Freud was primarily responsible for this theory, and it has continued with substantial modifications over a number of years. Although it originated in medicine, its influence has been felt in many areas of counseling.

Freud's insistence that the unconscious forces were the major contributors to neuroses aroused considerable criticism. However, this concept, although not fully accepted, has still made many therapists more aware of the possible influence of unconscious forces upon behavior and maladjustment. Appropriate modifications and adaptions have been made in this theory in an effort to utilize those elements found to be acceptable in today's society.

Humanistic psychology

Bruce (1966) places a number of theories, or partial theories, under the classification of humanistic psychology. This classification includes the following groups:

1. Neo-Freudian. Man is regarded as primarily social and cultural rather than biological and instinctual.

2. Gestalt or Field. Interaction with the environment must be considered in its totality.

3. Organismic. This stresses the need to consider the individual as a whole.

4. Perceptual. This emphasizes the uniqueness and importance of the individual, and his ability to do for himself.

It is under the umbrella of humanistic psychology that many of the current theories have found shelter and have flourished. The ideas espoused and the concepts developed have found favor with many therapists and counselors in medical and educational settings. The influence of this psychology can be expected to continue and become increasingly influential as new elements and ideas are developed.

Related forces

A number of other theoretical forces have made an impact on counseling theory. Some representative ones include ego-counseling (Hummel 1962), which, as the author suggests, is "elusive to define" (p. 463). It incorporates a number of approaches into a rather broad framework designed to initiate and perpetuate client growth. Dreyfus (1967) builds a case for "humanness" as an important variable underlying all successful therapeutic approaches. The research cited suggests that it is the quality of the human relationship that brings therapeutic value to the client, rather than any particular technique.

Ideas, experimentation, and imagination are all essential to the development of useful counseling approaches. We should continue to build upon and extend current knowledge, hopeful of discovering and developing something better than that currently in existence. It is this attitude that constitutes the principal motivating force behind counseling, as described in this text. This concept of counseling welcomes all ideas that may have practical application possibilities or that may stimulate further thought toward more significant developments in counseling.

Summary

A theoretical framework from which to function in counseling is most essential. The guidelines provided within such a framework ensure a systematic approach and avoid the inefficiencies and ineffectiveness of a haphazard and unorganized approach.

A theory lends practicality to an approach as it permits the use of logical and realistic techniques by the counselor. Theory gives sense and meaning to what the counselor does. The need for theory as a guide in counseling is quite evident.

There are three main theoretical forces underlying current theories. These are associationism, classical psychoanalysis, and humanistic psychology. It is from these that a number of related theories have been developed.

Study and discussion problems

1. Identify the possible advantages and disadvantages of a counselor's observing one theory only in his work.
2. Explain the relationship between a knowledge of theory and a counselor's effectiveness.
3. Reconcile through explanations any persisting discrepancies between theory and practice.
4. Explain or give an example of how a counselor might apply a concept gained from theory.

5. Diagram a structure that could be used in defining theory.
6. We are told that there is still a great need for a counseling theory for young children. Identify some important implications for this condition.
7. Explain what generally happens in the development of a theory.
8. Name and briefly describe each of the main theoretical forces in psychology that underlie counseling and psychotherapy.

/ 3 /

Traditional psychoanalytic theory

Traditional psychoanalytic theory had its beginning with Sigmund Freud, who was born of Jewish parentage in Moravia in 1856 and died in London of cancer of the jaw in 1939. He had a long and eventful career in Vienna with psychoanalysis as his major pursuit.

Freud's ambitious and illustrious career was marked by a great number of publications, most of which were reports of his findings and observations, based upon his work as a psychotherapist. Many of his beliefs and conclusions were revolutionary for his time. A number of these persist, and they provide a framework of operation for therapists throughout the world. Some of Freud's theories have been rejected, some accepted, and others have been modified. Many psychotherapists have followed the pattern of thought established by Freud, and his influence has been keenly and widely felt.

Background

In view of Freud's family life, medical training, and professional experiences, it is easy to understand his point of view on medical matters. The encouragement received from his merchant father and devoted mother gave impetus to Freud's brilliance and driving ambitions. His training in medicine and the biological sciences contributed to his insistence upon the influence of body functioning upon psychological functioning.

His deterministic point of view led to the conclusion that even the simplest behavior had an antecedent somewhere in the unconscious. Man, therefore, was essentially unaware of the causes underlying his conduct, although such causes did exist.

Freud's failures to convince his colleagues at various times on some elements of his beliefs appear to have only increased his determination to prove himself right. Much of the good to come from Freud's efforts is found in the thinking and contributions of many of Freud's dissenters. Disagreement has prompted some profound thought and probing research, which have markedly contributed to developments in psychotherapy.

Major theoretical elements

The main theoretical elements of the psychoanalytic approach are basic to the personality development of the individual, and they set the course for behavior. Man is seen as something of a victim of internal forces over which he has little control. His greatest hope lies in being able to control these forces through self-discipline and assistance from the environment.

Guiding forces in man's life

1. Unconscious forces. The unconscious mental processes underlie maladjustment and maladaptive behavior, and the symptoms are derived from the unconscious (Sahakian 1969). This unconscious level of the mind makes up the bulk of human personality, and the source of many of man's adjustment problems is thus traced to the unconscious. The purpose of therapy is to expose and identify those events or conditions that have a direct relationship with the individual's symptoms and current maladjustment.

2. Structure of personality. The three major systems of the id, ego, and superego provide an explanation for behavior. The id is the basic component of the personality and expresses the true purpose of the individual organism, which is the satisfaction of its innate needs. It is the reservoir of psychic energies and instinctual impulses that constantly demand expression. It represents the inner world of experience in which pain is avoided and pleasure is sought. Its basic function is to maintain the organism in a state of comfort and low tension (Hansen, Stevic, and Warner 1972). An unrestrained id produces pleasure-seeking, self-centered behavior. Left unchecked, it causes a rift between the individual and his society, a situation that frequently leads to serious consequences.

The ego is the intermediary force between the id and the environment. It attempts to reduce tension by finding an appropriate object for satisfying a need. Flexibility is required as the ego is constantly and alertly attempting to reconcile the differences between the inner, and even savage, wishes of the individual and the more tempered expectations of society. The ego is the disciplinary force by which the individual manages to stay out of trouble.

The superego is partly one's conscience and partly the imposed values of one's parents. The development of the superego occurs primarily through the process of identification with the parents. The infant learns early that the objects in his external world upon which he must depend for need fulfillment are his parents. He also learns rather quickly the acceptability or unacceptability of certain behaviors through a system of rewards and punishments provided by his discipline-oriented parents.

The superego, then, is an internal psychic energy that gradually replaces the parents as a directive force and that dictates behavior by calling one to account for his deeds and thoughts, and even for his unexecuted intentions (Sahakian 1969). The superego is, in a fashion, an heir to the Oedipus complex, which has been a source of guilt feelings for the boy because of the sexual attraction he has felt for his mother, or the Electra complex, which has been a source of guilt feelings for the girl—she has blamed her mother for her lack of a penis and has felt guilt for her attraction to her father. The severity of the superego is frequently experienced by one whose behavior is inconsistent with the coercive forces from his past.

The superego, according to Freud, really has two major systems: (1) the conscience, which represents those things the individual believes he should not do; and (2) the ego-ideal, which represents those things the individual would like to be. The inevitability of some conflict between each of these forces and the id impulses is plainly seen. Some compensation for possible guilt is found in the sense of satisfaction experienced by the individual as he pleasurably responds to his internal drives.

3. Instincts. Behavior occurs in the individual as a result of two kinds of events. These are situational events, or environmental stimuli, and instinctual drives, or innate psychological energies. The instinctual drives provide much of the force underlying behavior. First, there are the drives that result from biological functioning and that are expressed as quantities of energy that vary in intensity and pressure. Second, there is eros or life instinct, comprised of the self-preservative drive and sexual energy, which Freud termed the libido. Third, there is thanatos or the death instinct, which is opposed to the self-preservative drive and represents the organism's attempt to return to a previous neutral state.

The accumulation of psychological energy must be reduced through one of the following methods: primary process, secondary process, or a habitual or repetitive response. Primary process is related to the principle of homeostasis and implies an undirected effort at tension reduction to a neutral point. It is pleasure seeking, and it desires immediate gratification. Secondary process is the means by which tension reduction is accomplished in a thoughtful, rational manner. It implies the ego control of activity and is a function of the reality principle.

The third response category, the habitual response, is used to explain the fact that not all responses are directed tension reduction. Some responses, for example, may serve to generate increased tension such as that associated with sexual responses.

4. Aggression and the sex drive. The psychological energies of aggression and the sex drive contribute markedly to man's conduct. Man is, then, a victim of his own internal and relatively uncontrollable forces. External forces are essential to his acceptance and well-being within society. Some self-discipline and environmental deterrents are called for to combat these internal, psychological energies.

5. Growth stages. The five psychosexual stages through which the child moves are instrumental in prompting certain behaviors (Hansen, Stevic, and Warner 1972). (1) The first year of life is characterized by the *oral stage,* in which the child experiences the pleasurable sensation found in sucking. Just as important as the food intake achieved is the equally satisfying sensation found in sucking. Later, during this stage of development, a new phase occurs as the child finds that biting and chewing offer him a new way to relate to others. It is during this period that Freud saw aggressive and destructive impulses developing. The end of the oral period is characterized by a weaning process that Freud related to the potential for sadistic behavior.

(2) The *anal stage* finds the child during his second year shifting to the anal zone of the body as a source of pleasant sensations. Satisfaction is found in the elimination function, and in a later phase of development, in the retention of feces. Strict toilet training may result in the child's refusing to eliminate as a means for getting even. A fixation at this stage, or any of the other stages, may contribute markedly to personality problems throughout life.

(3) The *phallic stage* occurs approximately between the ages of three and six, and it finds the child sufficiently mature to gain pleasure from the manipulation of his sex organs. The latter part of this stage is characterized by the Oedipus complex, in which the boy experiences a desire to possess his mother, and the Electra complex, in which the girl wishes to possess her father. Of significance to later development is the child's resolution of the castration complex, or anxiety. The discovery that boys have a penis, and that girls do not, may create fear in the boy that the sexual attraction he feels toward his mother may result in castration. The resolution of this dilemma is achieved through the boy's

successful identification with the powerful male figure of his father. The discovery by girls that they have no penis may prompt a "penis envy," and may initially lead to a dislike of the mother and an attraction to the father. The process of resolving this problem is again through identification with the same-sexed parent, and after girls have accepted their biological differences from boys.

(4) The *latency period* is one of relative calm, from about the age of six to pre-adolescence, during which the child gives considerable attention to skill development. This is a period in which the primacy of the sexual drive lessens and the child enters a less dramatic stage of development. However, successful transition through this stage and its importance to later development are a result of the mastery of, or the successful progress through, prior stages.

(5) The *genital stage* comes at the onset of puberty, and it provides the adolescent with fuel for possible problems. He experiences strong biological drives, closely associated with sexual development, which must be sublimated for the most part if he is to conform to society's expectations. This is the final stage preliminary to adulthood and maturity.

6. *The nature of man.* Man is basically evil and the victim of instincts, a condition that must be reconciled with social forces. His best hope rests with his ability to achieve and maintain an appropriate balance between his internal impulses and the external restrictions imposed by reality and society. Achieving this balance is a matter of deep understanding of the impulses or forces that motivate the individual to action. The analyst is the authority, or skilled practitioner, who helps the individual overcome his weaknesses. He renders rational the irrational and is able to uncover the hidden depths of the unconscious (Carkhuff and Berenson 1967).

Techniques in psychotherapy

Although a number of techniques characterize this theory, central to all of these is a talking out by the patient. He talks about events that elicit emotional responses. The therapist then focuses upon the possible meaning of these events and explains their relevance to current maladjustments. The therapist's reactions to the patient's talk are marked by an assumption that a change in speech behavior can lead to a modification of the thought processes. Therapy emphasizes the concept of transference, in which the patient transfers his feelings to the parent-surrogate therapist. Free association and dream analysis are devices used by the therapist to penetrate the unconscious; in this way the patient may be directed toward those areas of concern by the knowledgeable therapist. Therapy, which is generally long term and time consuming, is not complete until the patient is no longer suffering from his symptoms, and it is assumed by the therapist that the patient will not regress since he has exposed so much formerly repressed material.

A critique of psychoanalytic theory

One's understanding of a theory can be increased and sharpened, and his own thinking broadened and deepened, through a critical look at existing theory. A clarification of vague or unexplained points is also possible. Such an exercise has the commendable outcome of a better educated individual, and one more adequately prepared to make his own impact upon thought and practice.

An attempt to identify the implications of each concept of a theory is likewise a profitable experience. This is the next step beyond becoming well acquainted with the concepts. Here, the individual's true understanding of the theory is put to the test, and his capacity for seeing the practical application possibilities of a concept is probed and challenged.

Certain questions, then, provide direction in identifying the elements within the theory and in ascertaining the implications of a theory for the counselor. What is the true meaning of each element, or concept, in the theory? What does the counselor do in response to each element considered? How does identifying the implications better the counselor's competence? These and other questions serve as guides as we consider the strengths and weaknesses of a theory. Hopefully, the answers to these problems are found as a critique is made of each element of a theory.

A response to psychoanalytic theory

It should be remembered that the influence of this theory has continued throughout the development of other theories and counseling approaches. Modifications have occurred as the various theorists have found better explanations for human behavior, and techniques have also been modified and new ones added. Although Freud rarely took kindly to criticisms of his ideas, such criticisms have been good for counseling and psychotherapy. The thought generated in an intelligent critique provides a beginning point for improvements in theory and practice. The next section is a critique of each of the main concepts of this theory.

1. Unconscious forces. Unconscious mental processes are undoubtedly potent forces in influencing and determining behavior, and they do contribute markedly to maladjustment and emotional problems. Rather than denying the existence of these forces, we could utilize them positively for the promotion of an individual's growth. They are not accepted as inevitable deterrents to behavior change or to better adjustments. Ways are sought to capitalize upon the positive aspects of these unconscious forces to the advantage of the individual. So, instead of man's becoming a victim of his past experiences and the resultant psychological impact they have, he minimizes their negative influence and capitalizes upon the positive elements present. The possibilities for positive influences are at least as great as the possibilities for negative influences.

The counselor's objective is to help the individual attain a level of self-understanding, including the unconscious psychological phenomena, that will permit a full utilization of all existing capacities and past experiences. No condition is tolerated as an inevitable barrier to growth and learning. The condition of unconscious forces is accepted only as a fact, an understanding of which increases its worth and reduces its harmful possibilities.

2. Structure of personality. Any system of personality, including the one that identifies the id, ego, and superego concepts, is acceptable as a means to a better understanding of human behavior. The fact that these elements of personality are biologically unintelligible makes them no less valuable. Our main interest is in attempting to fathom the complexities of the personality and to profit from the knowledge gained, so any explanations that further this objective have merit. We realize that the individual is an aggregate of complexities that normally defy description and explanation. Living with and capitalizing upon this notion is not difficult. The counselor's task is to help the individual toward a realization of his greatest potential. A full understanding of the personality is not essential to the attainment of this goal.

3. Instincts. Instincts are regarded as potentialities and psychic energies within the individual that demand expression. Since drives, desires, and ambitions prompt and motivate the individual to action, his chances for achievements are increased. Driving forces within the individual are essential to effective and meritorious achievements. To what extent these forces are, or depend upon, instinct is of minor importance. A recognition and acceptance of these psychological forces are made. The next step is one of so structuring our activities as to make full and productive use of these forces. Attempts are made to utilize these energies by integrating them with environmental forces for dynamic and productive action.

4. Aggression and the sex drive. Aggression and the sex drive, when seen as a desire to achieve, to be accepted, and to attain status, would be characterized as sublimation by Freud. This points up a significant difference in an interpretation of acceptable outlets for drives between the Freudian psychoanalytic therapist and other theoretical viewpoints. Aggression does not necessarily mean the venting of one's hostilities upon others, rather it may lead to an ambitious pursuit of goals. The sex drive has both biological and psychological components. The promptings felt by the mature adult toward sexual expression owe their origin to the ambition to achieve socially, to at least as great a degree as they do to glandular stimulation. These, then, are positive forces that, when properly channeled and enhanced, contribute markedly to one's achievements and add considerable zest to life, particularly as the intervention of the therapist has its impact.

So rather than being an unwilling victim of these forces, the individual is more dynamic, productive, and effective because of them. It is this view that created the rift between Freud and a number of his associates including Alfred Adler and Otto Rank. The person utilizes his aggressive tendencies positively for self-improvement and progress. The sex drive, irrespective of its exact origin, is utilized as a positive force, incentive, or motivation in influencing others, achieving goals, and realizing satisfactions in life.

5. Growth stages. The psychosexual stages of development are viewed as partial explanations for the growth process. The attempts to explain behavior on the basis of five developmental stages have merit to the degree to which they provide enlightenment about development. Agreement about the precise behavior to be expected of a child at a particular age is not necessary. For example, the knowledge that the infant's behavior is characterized by sucking, as a fulfillment to his eating and sensation needs, is sufficient. Whether or not there is a developmental stage at which the child gains satisfaction from elimination is relatively unimportant. It is important that he develop positive, wholesome attitudes toward himself and his bodily functions and that he learn certain controls and skills by which his physical needs may be met.

The general curiosity of the child about his physical self is natural and commendable. He may be no more curious about, or receive any more satisfaction from, exploring one part of his body than another. His attitude will reflect the attitude of the adults around him. A casual, understanding, matter-of-fact acceptance of all aspects of the developmental process should characterize the environment during the child's early years.

The "Oedipal conflict" and other phenomena of the traditional theory are seen as exaggerations and misinterpretations of a child's feelings. Obviously, a male child will feel close to his mother and have a deep affection for her. The fact that he may feel some sexual attraction for her is only a manifestation of the appeal he may see in most warm, accepting females. The fact that his mother may be the object of his sexual fantasies is understandable in view of his limited experiences and the fact that biological promptings trigger such fantasies and dreams. Other females are also the center of his attention during these times. The fact that the little girl may feel a special attraction for her father likewise calls for no particular concern.

The prepubertal and pubertal periods of growth are characterized by an intensification of sexual feelings, prompted by biological changes and social expectations. Whether or not abnormalities in behavior result depends to a great extent upon the quality of instruction he receives and upon the attitudes of adults around him. During this time, the growing child needs additional information about himself and kindly, understanding acceptance. It is a time to be anticipated and joyfully accepted because of the promise this maturing holds for a richer and fuller life.

6. The nature of man. The nature of man is essentially good, promising, and hopeful as seen by growth counseling. Man has the inherent potentialities for developing positively, wholesomely, and worthily. The potentialities for evil are also present, but to a much lesser degree. It is difficult to identify evil in a newborn child, while the qualities of innocence, warmth, and appeal are very much in evidence. Only through the most unfavorable of environmental conditions will the growing infant or child find positive reinforcement for evil, and only through environmental manipulation is this normally accomplished.

We thus assume the presence of goodness and the possibilities for greatness in each child. Any wrongdoing of which he may become guilty is attributable to his efforts to adjust to inappropriate circumstances in his environment and not to any inherent badness.

A promise for better theory

The greatest possibilities for the development of new and better counseling theory rest with a proper utilization of present theory. The complete abandonment of the present theories as a step in developing new theories would be unrealistic. Progress and improvement are based upon present knowledge, with newness and innovations being primarily extensions of the now. Experience, observation, and research help in a determination of the most and the least promising elements of each theory. The best elements are thus used, modified, or amplified, and a sound structure for counseling is developed. New ideas are then added to permit an extension of knowledge into the unknown, which must then be explored and extended. Theory thus becomes a combination of the past, present, and future. New theory becomes a reality and a promise for more exciting and effective counseling approaches.

The psychoanalytic approach is an example of this process. It was the forerunner of other theories, as it provided a beginning point and plotted a course for most counseling and psychotherapy.

Even the unacceptable elements have served a useful purpose, as they contributed to the need for more intensive experimentation. The knowledge gained has resulted in a renewed impetus to counseling approaches.

Criticizing a theory provides benefits for the individual so engaged, as it permits a greater understanding of the theory and stimulates the mental processes from which more profound thought may emerge.

Summary

The psychoanalytic theory provided the background from which many other theories have emerged, some of which have been in agreement and some in disagreement. Freud, as the pioneer in this movement, has been a dynamic force in the development of psychoanalysis.

The major elements of this theory include attempts to explain behavior and to provide treatment for individuals experiencing psychological problems.

A more modern view of the concepts of this theory stresses the notion that the individual need not be a victim of his past or the psychological forces within him. A full utilization of the potential held by one's environment and one's own internal resources is the key to one's adjustment and effective functioning.

Study and discussion problems

1. Describe as well as you can Sigmund Freud as an individual.
   a. Identify the highlights of his life.
   b. Describe the relationship you see between events and conditions in his life and the psychoanalytic theory.
   c. Describe how he might react to some of the more current counseling theories.
2. Enumerate each of the main elements of the psychoanalytic theory, and give a brief description of each.
3. Identify what you regard as the strengths and limitations of each of the elements, and defend your views.
4. Identify those parts of the critique with which you feel you can agree, and defend your position.
5. Identify those parts of the critique with which you would take issue, and defend your position.
6. Enumerate the greatest contributions of this theory to counseling and psychotherapy.

References

Corsini, R., ed. 1973. *Current psychotherapies.* Itasca, Illinois: F. E. Peacock. Pp. 1–33.

Ford, D. H., and Urban, H. B. 1963. *Systems of psychotherapy.* New York: John Wiley and Sons. Pp. 109–178.

Hansen, J. C., Stevic, R. R., and Warner, R. W. 1972. *Counseling: Theory and process.* Boston: Allyn and Bacon. Pp. 26–38.

Patterson, C. H. 1966, 2nd ed., 1973. *Theories of counseling and psychotherapy.* New York: Harper and Row. Pp. 303–335 (1966); Pp. 245–277 (1973).

Shertzer, B., and Stone, S. C. 1968, 2nd ed., 1974. *Fundamentals of counseling.* Boston: Houghton Mifflin Company. Pp. 205–214.

/ 4 /

Individual psychology

Individual psychology is frequently referred to as "Adlerian psychology," after Alfred Adler, its founder and strongest advocate. This approach has a long and successful history, which has included its adoption by many counselors and psychotherapists. It has been particularly popular as an approach in family counseling, with Rudolph Dreikurs its leading exponent.

Background

Alfred Adler was born of Jewish parentage in 1870 in Vienna and later became a well-known and highly respected psychiatrist. He spent considerable time in the United States from 1926 until his death in 1937. He and Freud were well acquainted, and although they had some serious differences in views, which eventually led to their parting company, each still had a deep and profound respect for the other professionally.

Adler consistently opposed the idea that he was ever a student of

Freud's, but he did admit to a close professional relationship with Freud. The fact that he was fourteen years younger, and not nearly as well known as Freud, suggests that he no doubt capitalized upon the advantage that such an association had for his own professional advancement. Many of Adler's ideas and theories were developed as a protest against some of Freud's theories that Adler found unacceptable.

Major theoretical elements

Although some elements of this theory oppose the psychoanalytic theory, there are others that in reality have a foundation in the psychoanalytic theory. Efforts were made by Adler and others to identify the real reasons for maladaptive behavior. Instead of blaming the past and attempting to identify events in one's life that triggered the difficulties, Adlerian psychology attributes much of man's behavior to his desire to achieve status in his society.

Forces underlying behavior

The individual is neither the victim of his unconscious forces nor the complete master of himself. There are indeed forces that help to shape his behavior. There are also philosophical points underlying this theory that give it meaning and set a course for the techniques to be used (Dreikurs 1968; Dimick and Huff 1970).

Basic to this theory is the belief proposed by Adler that two main conditions prompted the development of abnormal behavior. One of these came from the feelings of inferiority experienced by the individual early in life. The second was that, in his attempt to deal with these overwhelming feelings of inferiority, the individual developed inappropriate patterns of behavior (Hansen, Stevic, and Warner 1972). He further proposed that the individual with a physical handicap, or one who may be neglected by parents, might well develop strong feelings of inferiority.

One's feelings of inadequacy thus had an origin in the attitude of the person concerning his biological inferiority. The notion that he was biologically inadequate and thus less competent than others prompted a strong feeling of being biologically inferior.

The basic postulates of this theory give it philosophical and psychological structure that may be utilized in counseling. These same postulates may serve as beginning points for modifications in the theory or for the development of new postulates.

1. A social being. Since man is essentially and inherently a social being, his actions are prompted by a desire to achieve a position of importance in his society. Behavior is thus attributable to these urges to be socially acceptable and to maintain a position of status with others. It is these urges that stimulate the individual to action, and not the sexual urges, as was Freud's contention. Sexual urges exist, but with a close association with the need to find satisfaction in the social setting.

2. The lifestyle. Man's strivings are in response to his own creative capacities and to his basic need for experiences that will enhance his unique lifestyle. This style develops early in life as the child experiences successes and failures in his trial-and-error efforts to ensure his acceptance. Behaviors that bring a positive response from others are repeated, while those that fail in this objective are dropped. Persistent failure in one's attempts to please and to be accepted brings frustration, which may trigger deliberate antisocial behavior.

3. Combination of sociability, acceptability, and independence. Man is primarily a social creature, but he still maintains a degree of uniqueness that permits a sense of independence essential to his own sense of dignity and importance. The goal sought is one of pleasing others while still functioning with sufficient autonomy to feel independent and uncontrolled. This permits an attitude of importance, particularly if the admiration of others is gained at the same time.

4. Conscious forces. Consciousness, not unconsciousness (Freudianism), is really the potent force behind behavior. The individual is very much aware of himself and of his surroundings and is therefore able to exercise appropriate controls. The elements in himself are essentially at the conscious level and are within the grasp of his understanding. Any unconscious forces at work are of relatively little consequence in dictating behavior.

   5. Normality and health. The focus of concern is upon normality and health, not upon illness and abnormality (Christensen 1969). Maladaptive behavior has its origin in a lack of knowledge, information, or experience, and calls for treatment that will correct these deficiencies. The promotion of good mental health through avoidance techniques as well as treatment thus receives constant attention.

   The desire to please others prompts a movement toward them and the initiation of actions designed to please. If one's efforts are rewarded by the positive responses of others, he will continue in these actions. A rebuff causes anxiety and creates the need for more acceptable behavior. The interpretation he places upon a failure is instrumental in determining subsequent behavior. He evaluates himself on the basis of his successes and failures, and he makes certain conclusions, sometimes erroneous, as to the approaches to be used for successful social living. Maladaptive behavior may then occur as incorrect approaches to gaining and maintaining status in a group. The individual's interpretation thus fosters the inappropriate behavior, not the actual situation.

   6. Purpose of behavior. All behavior has a purpose and is an effort to meet some essential need of the individual. This purpose is generally one of finding a suitable place for oneself in the social setting (Grubbe 1968). Achieving this place depends upon one's self-confidence and a positive self-concept. This condition provides the impetus for approaching tasks positively and for the development of skills needed for healthy social interaction. The individual's withdrawal from social settings often occurs as a response to feelings of insecurity and inadequacy. This reaction then lays the groundwork for continuing maladaptive behavior, which cannot possibly meet his social needs. Inappropriate behavior then becomes a defense mechanism, while at the same time contributing to the alienation of other people, whose acceptance and approval he so desperately needs. He will continue to act, however, in attempts to meet his needs. Each act has a purpose and a meaning, carrying with it a hope for success.

7. Perceptions and behavior. Perceptions play an important part in behavior, as the individual tends to behave in a fashion consistent with his perception of the situation. Most individuals have some justification for feeling inadequate and insecure. The reason for feelings of inferiority may be due to size, appearance, ability, socioeconomic standing, intelligence, or family. Whatever the reason, the condition is not as important as the person's attitude toward it. How he perceives the situation in respect to himself is the important factor. An erroneous perception or a faulty interpretation of the reactions of others may trigger inappropriate behavior, which only aggravates the individual's situation and intensifies his problems. Needed behavior changes are then achieved through helping the individual change his perceptions of himself or of the environment.

8. Competition and discouragement. Competition may be growth promoting if used appropriately. It may be, however, a serious deterrent to growth if it is perceived as unfriendly or unfair, thereby contributing to discouragement and other negative reactions. Encouragement is so essential to the successful progress of the individual (Dinkmeyer and Dreikurs 1963) that any suggestion to the contrary should be avoided.

9. Goals of disturbing behavior. Disturbing or inappropriate behavior has four main goals (Dreikurs 1968): (1) attention getting, (2) power, (3) revenge, and (4) withdrawal. In his attempts to gain social status, the individual resorts to behavior that he thinks will be most likely to achieve this goal. He deliberately behaves in a fashion designed to attract attention. When this happens with a child, a power struggle with an adult is likely to occur. It may also happen between adults. The thwarting of one's efforts to meet a social need may trigger some aggressive or violent behavior. Revengeful behavior may occur when the individual strongly resents the interference of another person in his efforts toward fulfillment.

Withdrawal denotes a giving up and a lack of willingness to carry on the battle. The individual prefers the abandonment of a goal and a condition of unfulfilled needs to the suffering experienced through continuing failures and rebuffs.

Tools and techniques of counseling

Flexibility in the use of various tools and techniques characterizes the efforts of the counselor. The goal is the identification of inappropriate behaviors, followed by plans to make needed changes. The decisions reached involve both the counselor and the client, but considerable responsibility is assumed by the counselor. He makes some definite suggestions about how the client can make behavior changes and how the client can best conduct himself in order to win social approval.

Some of the tools used include consultation, instruction, information giving, advising, and telling (Christensen 1969). The counselor focuses upon helping the individual see the true nature of his behavior and upon insisting that the client exert the necessary effort to effect changes. He does not concern himself unduly about the permissiveness of the relationship or the good will of the client.

Techniques include any one or any combination of several activities. These are: group counseling, informal group discussion, individual counseling, role-playing, and teaching. The client soon learns to take part in several settings, and he finds himself involved with other people as well as the counselor.

A leisurely naturalness characterizes the counseling relationship since long-term growth is an objective. The approach is problem-centered to a degree, but not crisis-centered. The selection of techniques is motivated by the desire to have them well integrated and in harmony with the principles of development. Individual needs are seen as parts of developmental needs.

Techniques also include working closely with teachers, parents, and other significant adults (Hillman 1967). The counselor helps the teacher understand himself and his feelings toward the child. Parents are also helped to a better understanding of the child, and suggestions are made on how to achieve the agreed upon goals. It is felt that adults close to the child must be a part of the therapy and planning sessions in order to achieve the most favorable results.

Any environmental manipulation is essentially one of helping people to change their perceptions of each other and of the environment and of devising more appropriate behaviors. Little attention is given to attempting to overcome inevitable environmental limitations. The individual is challenged to try new behaviors that are likely to be more rewarding than the behaviors that may be causing his difficulties. He is helped to see, for example, that crowding into a line is ultimately far less rewarding and appealing to his peers than politely moving to the end of the line.

The counselor is observant and alert to the meaning of behavior in a social setting (Grubbe 1968). While the concern of the teacher may, of necessity, be limited to seeing the child improve his behavior, the counselor may then give attention to the possible causes. For example, poor academic work may be due to a student's negative interpretation of his social environment. The counselor may then assist the child toward a more realistic and positive interpretation of that environment. The child with neurotic symptoms is helped to reduce or eliminate them through counseling techniques that reveal the symptoms as distorted interpretations of life.

Significant aspects of the child's environment are in focus during counseling sessions, some of which include other family members. An awareness of existing conditions is regarded as essential for any adjustment to and a proper interpretation of these conditions.

A critique of individual psychology

This theory has a number of sound and well-supported elements. It has enjoyed considerable success as a counseling approach, particularly with children in a school or home setting and with families. Its popularity will no doubt continue to grow as it continues to help individuals and families improve their effectiveness and better their adjustments.

A response to individual psychology

In responding to this theory, each element outlined earlier in the chapter is considered. The responses are essentially in agreement, but they also include some criticisms that call for possible improvement or extensions of the element.

The merits of this psychology are quite evident as they include encouraging behavior that will permit self-actualization and that will meet the expectations of the society. The desirability of man's striving for social acceptability through productivity and achievements has much to recommend it.

1. A social being. Man is, indeed, very much a social being, and much of his behavior denotes the concern he has for a positive association with others and for gaining social approval. The feelings of the individual are very much the same whether they are essentially inherent or environmentally motivated. The notion that feelings are motivated primarily by the environment has greater merit. A child adopts a form of behavior because it appears to have been successful with another person. Certain self-imposed, disciplinary controls are thus generated by the individual in order to conduct himself in a fashion acceptable to his society and in harmony with his own sense of decency. He is not, then, a victim of inherent drive for social approval, but rather a master of himself and his behavior. He learns to attract and to profit from social contacts, but as an outcome of controlled, acceptable behavior. Behavior is engaged in wisely as a means to personal satisfaction and pride, from which social approval may logically follow, not as a stilted means to a hoped for end.

It is understandable that the individual is concerned about his social status. His needs for feelings of importance and self-respect are fulfilled through the reactions of other people. It is through his associations and interactions that he gains this sense of importance. A failure to receive favorable responses will inevitably lead to an intensification of efforts to please, or to a withdrawal, or other maladaptive behavior.

2. The lifestyle. The concept of a lifestyle has merit as it encourages creativity and uniqueness. The qualities of independence and of strength of character are stressed here. A sense of pride and a confidence in one's own integrity should logically take precedence over social approval, and are stressed in growth counseling. The latter is desirable, but never as a compromise with oneself on what one feels is most important. The conduct fostered by the desire for social approval may be highly conforming only for the sake of conformity, since this is the way to please others.

A sense of independence is most essential to one's personal welfare, and it is logical to assume that this may be achieved without a break with or even the irritation of society. In fact, society admires independence, self-confidence, and strength. The very qualities that are needed by the individual for his best good are also the qualities that others admire. So, as the individual strives toward logical self-actualization, he is simultaneously evoking the plaudits of his social group.

The importance of an individual's learning to combine his own qualities and strengths with those of the society should be constantly stressed. Personal fulfillment and status with the society are thus complementary forces and should never be antagonistic.

3. Combination of sociability, acceptability, and independence. Sociability, acceptability, and independence are all-important goals of individual psychology. We can see the tendencies of the individual to attract attention and to find favor with others as desirable, if the approaches used are positive and self-fulfilling and free of inappropriate or self-demeaning compromises.

The counselor, then, recognizes the person's need for social involvement, and he helps him find and develop legitimate behaviors for meeting this need. The individual is also helped to recognize and capitalize upon the strengths within himself. He thus avoids any capitulation to societal pressures or to his own weaknesses as he finds his capacities sufficiently adequate to meet life's challenges. These same capacities become stronger through successful experiences and increasing self-confidence.

4. Conscious forces. Unconscious forces are given only minor heed in individual psychology. This was a point of contention between Adler and Freud. We, likewise, can see the need to stress the place of conscious forces as determinants of behavior. The inevitability, though not undesirability, of the unconscious is accepted, but with the belief that any negativism from the unconscious may be controlled through a better utilization of the conscious forces. The picture of the individual as a helpless victim of unseen forces is not acceptable.

We can see a relationship between the unconscious and behavior. These forces no doubt trigger certain actions, and they also discourage certain behavior. An awareness of this fact is useful as it encourages the individual to muster any needed conscious forces to offset any threatening negative influence. Self-discipline and appropriate self-controls are thus encouraged as the individual masters the unwanted unconscious forces and fully utilizes the conscious ones. The proper channeling of energies and drives is thus achieved as a goal of counseling with a highly motivated individual.

5. *Normality and health.* Normality and health are the focus of all counseling approaches designed to prevent maladjustments. Individual psychology is not unique in this position. We should recognize, however, an obligation to every individual found at the various levels of mental health. Since the emphasis is upon strengthening capacities and encouraging needed behavior changes, each person is accommodated according to his own individual needs. Each normal, healthy individual is aided in recognizing and developing his potentialities, and each person demonstrating symptoms of maladjustment is provided appropriate treatment. Referral to a clinician may be one of the counselor's principal functions here.

The desire to please others is commendable and normal, but the motivation to please and to accommodate oneself should be equally persuasive. Efforts are made in counseling to help the individual keep anxieties low and minimize undue concerns over any apparent nonacceptance by others. A healthy striving to meet one's needs and satisfy one's self should result in behavior that is also acceptable to others.

6. *Purpose of behavior.* Behavior is recognized as being purposeful and having meaning for the individual. However, this is an oversimplification of an important concept. The fact that the individual views his behavior as purposeful doesn't necessarily make it so. His reasoning may be illogical or he might grossly misinterpret a situation, which in turn

triggers the behavior. Certainly, the individual should be guided in his thinking and given considerable opportunity to probe the depth of his own intellect and emotions. Calm, logical thought should lead to intelligent decisions about how a person should behave and what behaviors hold the greatest promise for both meeting needs and pleasing others.

There is a need, then, to help the person recognize the real purpose behind his behavior, assisting him in reinforcing behaviors that will achieve the purpose and eliminating those with little promise for doing so. He can be taught to modify, abandon, or substitute for a purpose, once it is found to be inappropriate. For example, if the true purpose is to attract attention, he can be shown acceptable behaviors that will do this and can be encouraged in avoiding poor behavior. Insights, logical reasoning, and appropriate controls are utilized here.

The inevitability of certain driving forces that victimize the individual is not acceptable. Internal forces are recognized as having positive value as they are combined with societal expectations and as they are channeled for constructive outcomes.

7. Perceptions and behavior. Perceptions are influential in determining the nature of behavior, as the individual reacts in accordance with the way in which he sees and interprets a situation. However, the person really has considerable control over his perceptions, through the exercise of any needed self-discipline and the utilization of his intelligence. He can be helped to see why he perceives a situation as he does and to eliminate any errors in judgments. He can also be taught to avoid erroneous thinking and those biases that deter logic and positive action. This may be done best by providing for the development of positive attitudes toward incidents, events, and people. This fostering of appropriate perceptions, congruent with the facts, thus becomes a way of thinking and opens the way for positive, fruitful action.

There is, then, nothing final about one's initial perceptions of a situation. They are immediately subject to modification through logically imposed controls and effective counseling. The anticipation of appropriate perceptions and the avoidance of inappropriate ones thus become goals for the individual made·possible through counseling.

8. Competition and discouragement. The discouragement frequently encountered through unfair kinds of competition is a serious deterrent to growth and effective behavior. We can view the problem as essentially one of the frequent use of competition to the disadvantage of the individual. A competitive situation is used in growth counseling in a manner consistent with the personal needs and to the advantage of the competitors. Stress is given to the activity itself and to the joy found in involvement. The outcomes are relatively unimportant, and each person is permitted the satisfaction of knowing that his efforts have produced results. This avoids the possible disappointments and frustrations frequently fostered by failure.

The knowledge that successes are essential to one's well-being is used by the counselor in helping the individual realize positive feelings from his experiences. Proper attitudes toward "failures" are fostered through counseling, and through the promotion of a variety of experiences for the individual. Possible courses of action are considered, and the individual's strengths are identified and used in following through on choices. The person learns that there really is no such thing as failure, that this is only an attitude. Confidence is gained through action and involvement, and the possibilities for discouragement are reduced.

9. Goals of disturbing behavior. The goals of disturbing conduct, as outlined in individual psychology, are useful as they help to explain human behavior. These goals need not be undesirable, however, if they are achieved through appropriate behavior. For example, attention-getting conduct has a negative connotation. If the child's behavior is of this type, then he is being "bad" because "nice" people don't strive to attract attention.

In reality, the goal of attracting attention is a worthy and desirable one. It is through being noticed that the individual satisfies certain basic needs. To abandon this as a goal, just because the behavior used is sometimes disturbing, is to leave the individual with unfulfilled needs. It is preferable to leave attention-getting behavior as a goal but to concentrate efforts toward helping the individual develop his talents for legitimate behavior. Thus, any behavior engaged in holds the possibilities for personal satisfaction and pleasing others, and it also leads to other behaviors even more satisfying and productive. The individual's need for feeling important is met through appropriate activities, which also serve to please and attract others.

Revengeful behavior is abandoned as it fails to provide for personal satisfactions and as it evokes negative reactions from others. The individual is shown, and he practices, better ways of meeting needs. Withdrawal, likewise, becomes unrealistic behavior for him as it results in a failure to meet needs. It leads to unhappiness and dissatisfaction, rather than to the more realistic goals of success and progress.

Ways to improve this theory

Some important elements and concepts of individual psychology have been summarized. The many merits of this theory have been acknowledged, and support for them developed. Like all theories, possibilities for improvements become evident through careful study and analysis. The critique of this theory includes some differing points of view, which reflect the philosophy underlying a growth-counseling approach.

A fuller use of individual psychology rests with an extension of many of its existing concepts and with a more imaginative application of its principles. Counseling can more fully capitalize upon the concepts of man as a social being, the lifestyle, normality, purposefulness of behavior, and feelings of inadequacy. These are not to be accented as inevitable conditions over which there is little control, when in reality they are subject to the necessary controls and can be utilized as positive forces for effecting behavior changes and more productive action.

Summary

Individual psychology resulted from the efforts of Alfred Adler to provide more reasonable explanations for behavior than those postulated by Sigmund Freud. Adler's background of experiences with Freud contributed to an energetic attack upon the traditionalism of Freudianism and the successful development of another theory.

The main concepts of individual psychology stress the notion that man is essentially a social being and that his behavior is motivated by a desire to succeed within the society. Each individual develops a lifestyle at an early age as a way of behaving and of fulfilling needs.

Considerable importance is given to conscious forces, normality and health, the purposefulness of behavior, perceptions, and competition as major elements of this theory. The techniques of the counselor are broad and flexible and in keeping with the theoretical elements.

Growth counseling accepts many of the premises of individual psychology, but it also amplifies and extends many of these premises to a broader and more realistic framework of counseling. The limitations of individual psychology can be overcome by a more positive view of existing conditions and forces and by capitalizing upon those conditions and forces as positive influences in the lives of individuals.

Study and discussion problems

1. Describe Alfred Adler, both personally and professionally.
2. Identify the main points of difference between Adler and Freud.
3. Look at each of the nine points under the topic "Forces Underlying Behavior," and react.
   a. Note how and where you agree or disagree.
   b. Point out some important implications each point has for counseling.
4. Enumerate some of the major techniques employed in this form of counseling. Criticize each of these techniques in respect to its relationship to the philosophies of the theory.
5. Develop your own critique of the concepts underlying this theory.

References

Corsini, R., ed. 1973. *Current psychotherapies.* Itasca, Illinois: F. E. Peacock. Pp. 35–83.

Ford, D. H., and Urban, H. B. 1963. *Systems of psychotherapy.* New York: John Wiley and Sons. Pp. 304–365.

Hansen, J. C., Stevic, R. R., and Warner, R. W. 1972. *Counseling: Theory and process.* Boston: Allyn and Bacon. Pp. 54–74.

/ 5 /

Client-centered counseling

The client-centered approach is so designated because of the focus given to the individual being counseled and because of the freedom granted the individual for decision making. The approach centers upon the client and is structured to give him considerable responsibility in the relationship.

The "self theory" is the designation sometimes given to this approach, which is characterized by elements of the phenomenological and existential philosophies. Like most theories, the client-centered theory was strongly influenced by a philosophy concerning the nature of man. The techniques used in this approach reflect a philosophy and are used as a response to the philosophy. Certain beliefs thus contribute to how a client is treated and help determine how he can best be helped.

Background

Client-centered counseling owes its beginning to Carl R. Rogers, whose protests against conventional therapies resulted in some highly controversial notions about treatment procedures. He was particularly critical of the intervention concept in which the therapist exercised considerable control over the client. His theoretical ideas stressed counselor restraint and client responsibility, with the client's having considerable freedom in expressing himself and in determining how to deal with his problems.

Rogers has enjoyed a long and highly successful career. The years since his birth in 1902, and his formal education at the University of Wisconsin, Union Theological Seminary, and Columbia University, have been marked by a very exciting and productive career. His earliest writing efforts (Rogers 1942) were something of a protest against traditional psychotherapy. More recent publications (Rogers 1951; 1961) are confirmations of the belief that this therapy is characterized by tentativeness and that it has really been an ongoing process as much as a therapy (Seeman 1965). The theory was initially a result of Rogers's observations and curiosity, rather than an outcome of any clear-cut, empirically supported theory. Considerable research on the theory has added to its objectivity and reputation.

This theory shows the marks of battle, since its critics have been both numerous and verbal. It has, however, enjoyed considerable popularity, and the strong position of this theory among counselors and psychotherapists is well recognized. It continues as a rather flexible, open-ended, ever-expanding theory, marked by tentativeness and a tolerance for change.

Major theoretical elements

A number of theoretical elements characterize this theory as a result of the early questioning of the traditional beliefs and techniques. The nature of the therapist's role was one of the first questions posed. Rogers feels that true client growth comes from the client's own active involvement in the therapeutic process, rather than from the direction provided by the therapist. This notion calls for restraint by the therapist and an emphasis upon client autonomy. Feelings are given priority in the relationship, and reflecting these feelings is a major technique of the therapist. The idea here is to recognize and clarify feelings.

Main themes of this theory

The main themes of this theory (Ford and Urban 1963) include: (1) affective responses, (2) faith in the nature of man, (3) purposiveness of behavior, (4) client responsibility, and (5) science as observation.

Two related themes (Rogers 1951) are the beliefs that: (1) inherent in each individual is the capacity to understand relevant factors in his life, and (2) powers and capacities of the individual may be utilized more effectively by virtue of the counseling relationship.

The main function of the therapist is to provide a setting in which the client feels free to express himself and to explore the depths of his true feelings without fear or embarrassment. Since man is basically constructive and trustworthy, he will make better adjustments as he feels no need to be defensive (Patterson 1966). Greater self-actualization is achieved as the individual sees the possibilities within himself. Psychotherapy provides for a liberation of one's capacities, and growth occurs as insights are gained and as self-confidence improves.

Considerable faith rests in the therapist's observation of people. Significant trends are normally observed in the client (Rogers 1951). (1) He moves toward being more open to experience, and he tends to perceive himself more realistically and less fearfully. (2) He lives each moment more fully, and he sees himself as a process characterized by fluidity and change. (3) He becomes increasingly more trusting of himself, and he acts with confidence.

Techniques and tools of counseling

The techniques of this approach are implied and somewhat obvious to the counselor who understands the philosophies and concepts underlying this theory. It is through the application of these concepts that this approach makes its contribution to client and counselor (Carkhuff and Berenson 1967). The techniques used include an implementation of the counselor's philosophy and attitudes (Patterson 1966).

We find certain procedures to be fundamental and representative of this theory. (1) Reflection of feeling characterizes this approach and predominates as a technique. The counselor reflects in somewhat different terminology, but with accuracy, the feelings expressed by the client. (2) An attitude of careful listening with a genuine interest in the individual and an empathy for him is in evidence. (3) Considerable encouragement is directed to the client to express himself fully and completely. (4) The client's feelings are recognized, accepted, and clarified.

It is from these and related techniques that the goals of client-centered counseling are achieved. Augmenting the techniques is an atmosphere characterized by warmth, acceptance, and permissiveness.

Core concepts of client-centered counseling

Many of the concepts of this theory have been identified under previous topics. This section pinpoints more specifically the main concepts of the theory. While some of these are essentially philosophical, and others relate more particularly to techniques, no effort is made to separate the two.

1. Active involvement. A definite involvement in the therapeutic process is the key to client growth. While expressing his feelings, the individual is simultaneously developing and being a part of a relationship with the counselor. The processes of expressing feelings and thinking through problems have growth-promoting benefits.

2. Capacity for growth. Each person has the capacity to recognize and deal with relevant events and incidents. It is assumed that he has the intellectual and emotional resources needed to deal with problems and to profit from his experiences.

3. Growth through permissiveness. The counseling relationship is marked by warmth, understanding, and permissiveness. The client will be more likely to profit from the experience and take significant action if there is little structure or coercion. An atmosphere that provides for self-explanation and unrestricted movement is conducive to progress.

4. Basic goodness of man. Philosophically, man is regarded as basically good, constructive, and trustworthy. He is capable of self-actualization and will move positively as he senses the possibilities within himself. There is a genuine faith in man as a worthy, contributing, self-actualizing person.

5. Insight and change. The key to full functioning rests with the gaining of insights from which behavior changes may be made. The sense of freedom experienced in the relationship fosters the gaining of insights.

6. Independence and integration. A constant goal of counseling is the achievement of a sense of independence and a total integration of the individual's qualities. Independent action is viewed as increasing strength and improving competence. It suggests that the individual is better able to handle conflicts and is more fully utilizing his capabilities. An integration of abilities is essential to one's full functioning.

7. Focus upon the emotional or affective. The emotional aspects of the problem, or of the situation, are the focus of attention, with considerably less concern for the intellectual elements. How the person feels is the important consideration, not how he should feel or how the counselor thinks he should feel. The reflection of the feelings expressed is a common technique here.

8. The therapeutic benefits of counseling. The counseling contact and the activities found in the counseling relationship constitute a growth experience for the individual. The setting, the relationship developed, and the nature of the atmosphere serve to benefit the individual, apart from any formal, corrective technique used.

9. Client responsibility. The individual will profit most from counseling as he assumes considerable responsibility for his own actions, thoughts, and decisions. Growth occurs from the assumption of responsibility and not from being told or directed by someone else.

10. Counselor observations and feelings. The counselor's conclusions, based upon his observations and upon his feelings about a situation, carry considerable weight in the therapeutic process. Although the counselor does not impose his thinking upon a client, he still trusts his judgments about the person and about how to best help him. Empirical evidence has a place, but it is probably of less value than the counselor's more subjective judgment.

11. Tentativeness and tolerance. Tentativeness characterizes the approach as the client is given considerable freedom to think, feel, and act. The counselor is empathetic, accepting, and understanding in his efforts to encourage an expression of feeling. An absence of structure permits the client to explore in depth his feelings about a situation.

12. The irrationality of behavior. If the individual is acting irrationally, he will come to this conclusion through insight. Through the expression of feelings, he will eventually discover that his behavior is inappropriate and will then conclude that it should be changed. The insight, then, precedes any conscious efforts to change behavior.

A critique of client-centered counseling

This approach contains a number of philosophical and theoretical elements upon which many current theories have drawn. Some of the concepts are basic to virtually all counseling and therapeutic approaches. Differences in views also exist, thus resulting in some quite different concepts in some of the other theories.

Responses to this theory

The responses to each of the twelve concepts of the client-centered theory are influenced by two main conditions: (1) considerable agreement, and (2) attempts to minimize the limitations of this theory.

The growth-counseling approach utilizes many of the ideas of the client-centered approach, but it differs somewhat as it takes a more active and influential part in the therapeutic process. I would be reluctant to leave so much of the direction and initiative to a client who may be ill prepared to assume such responsibility. Growth counseling agrees with the necessity for a strong, positive working relationship and with the merit of having the individual assume considerable responsibility for the decisions made.

1. Active involvement. Active involvement in the therapeutic process is essential for client growth. This concept is readily accepted philosophically, but the nature of the involvement may vary considerably. It should not be limited just to expressing feelings, as is essentially the case under the client-centered approach. We can see this involvement as including considerable intellectualization on the part of client and counselor. Probing the depths of the intellect and objectively considering the evidence at hand are really augmenting influences that should hasten therapy and result in greater progress than the mere expression of feelings. Greater involvement by the counselor prevails as he helps to create a positive atmosphere in which mutual trust and respect are fostered. Full agreement on an issue is not always reached or even regarded as necessary. The client will come to know the feelings and attitudes of the counselor, but only as a means for improving his own understanding and not for the purpose of usurping his prerogatives. Total permissiveness and an absence of the counselor's views are not acceptable. The client is not left entirely to his own judgments, nor is he permitted to feel he has been abandoned in his need. The counselor takes an active part and is mildly assertive in helping to structure the relationship and in making proposals for possible courses of action.

2. Capacity for growth. The capacity for growth, that is, the ability to profit from counseling and to deal effectively with most problems, is a realistic condition with most people. However, since capacities vary considerably among individuals, and the motivation to utilize one's capacities is likewise variable, I feel the statement is an oversimplification. There is, then, a need for the counselor to be informed about the capacities of the client and also to be aware of the strength and nature of the individual's motives. In growth counseling, the individual is encouraged and expected to assume the responsibility for thinking, expressing his feelings, and decision making for which he is currently prepared. He is not, however, left to flounder in indecision, nor to waste time in a state of frustration. The counselor provides the direction necessary to help the individual assess and develop his capacities, improve his self-confidence, and learn new skills. His readiness for assuming more responsibility for himself and for making decisions is thus constantly increased.

3. Growth through permissiveness. Growth through permissiveness is possible with some, but not all, individuals. An atmosphere marked by warmth and acceptance is desirable for any counseling relationship, but a lack of structure may hinder the therapeutic process. Congeniality and fun are not the goals, but rather the goal should be action toward problem resolution. The atmosphere must be conducive to an in-depth intellectual and emotional consideration of the client's concerns.

The counselor's warm and accepting attitude has a place in counseling, as it permits essential structuring and provides meaningful action. Client growth is the real goal here, and it may be best achieved through a fairly direct approach once the goals are established. This warm, accepting attitude still exists as the counselor conveys the message that he understands and is willing to help. Some "directiveness" by the counselor need not detract from the congenial atmosphere if it is properly handled.

The unmotivated or immature individual is not likely to profit from a highly permissive atmosphere. Even the highly motivated or mature individual may, likewise, find the setting unrewarding if needed structure is lacking. A more structured, even abrupt, approach may best serve his needs, even at the risk of creating a less friendly atmosphere.

4. Basic goodness of man. The basic goodness of man is an acceptable concept, but with the assertion that the attributes that characterize goodness vary considerably with individuals. This being the case, treatment for different individuals should also vary. Environmental influences have caused some men to be less good and trustworthy and more evil than nature intended. So, in counseling, we must capitalize upon the inherent goodness of man and help each person avoid any tendencies to do evil.

Growth counseling utilizes assessment, subjective as it might be, for the purpose of determining the nature and extent of an individual's personal qualities and capacities. Assessment, then, provides information and makes possible a kind of planning essential to the individual's continuous program and worthy achievements. It is the intent to help each individual grow by whatever approach holds the greatest promise for him.

5. Insight and change. Insights are essential to meaningful and permanent changes in behavior and attitudes. Client-centered counseling sees the insight as a preliminary or forerunner to change. Growth counseling sees the necessity for insight but is more concerned with what happens following the insight. An insight's major function is to motivate the individual and to give impetus to his efforts to improve his effectiveness. It may be necessary to take some individuals through the actual steps of behavior change (behavior modification) before any insights occur. If no insight is gained, but the individual has, nevertheless, changed his behavior, this is still progress. Appropriate changes in behavior with no insight are preferable to no change in behavior. The ideal, of course, includes both.

Hopefully, insight will occur early in treatment, and the individual will adjust his actions accordingly. Once the individual sees the logic in an idea or the desirability of certain behavior, he is more likely to initiate the needed action than if there is no insight.

The counselor's position is one of promoting insight, and then augmenting it with encouragement for change. And, although insight depends upon intelligence and maturity, appropriate insight is still possible for the relatively dull or immature individual. Insight, like any action of the individual, must be at a level expedient for the person.

6. Independence and integration. Greater independence and a fuller integration of one's abilities are logical goals for any counseling approach. How much independence and how the term is defined by the individual are questions here. One's interpretation of "independence" and of "integration" must not be overlooked in counseling an individual.

Growth counseling accepts the concept of independence but stresses it as an integral part of one's total development, not as a goal to be achieved in isolation. The integration of capabilities is also seen as an important step in one's full functioning and as important to one's continuing growth. Increasing self-confidence and the improvement of skills are viewed as prerequisites to increasing independence and to a fuller integration of abilities.

7. Focus upon the emotional and affective. The focus upon the emotional or affective aspects of the problem has definite limitations for effective counseling. Growth counseling places no greater stress upon one than the other, viewing them as closely related, reciprocating forces in the person's life. How a person feels about a situation, a person, or even himself has a close relationship to his ability to profit from an experience. His intellectual capacities should also be utilized to the fullest in any serious consideration of a problem. As personal growth remains as the objective, emotional and intellectual elements are capitalized upon. The counselor's responses denote an awareness of and a need for both.

8. The therapeutic benefits of counseling. The therapeutic benefits of the counseling experience are contingent upon the suitability of the experience, depending upon how the client responds to and is permanently influenced by the experience. In other words, the key to the therapeutic value of the counseling experience rests with what the encounter triggers within the individual and how his behavior changes as a result of the counseling.

Internal growth is the outcome of any worthwhile experience. Verbal commitments, or some other external manifestation of a desire to please the counselor, are useless without a deep motivation and serious commitment to self-improvement. The internal capacities of the individual, and his character traits, denote growth from a fruitful experience. These are the characteristics upon which the individual must continue to rely for lasting and beneficial growth.

9. Client responsibility. An attitude of responsibility for self within counseling has merit. It is from such an attitude that a person will continue to profit from his experiences and draw appropriate conclusions. However, the imposition of responsibility for self upon the individual, without a due consideration for his readiness, and the anticipation of possible harmful effects could be devastating. It is the function of counseling to bolster self-confidence and to identify and utilize strengths, while still helping the individual overcome weaknesses. The building up of self, the bolstering of self-esteem, and the strengthening of self-confidence are areas of concentration in counseling. How much responsibility is left to the client depends upon his present status of confidence and skills and upon his willingness to assume such responsibility.

   10. Counselor observations and feelings. Counselor observations and feelings are not to be ignored, and they do carry considerable weight in the Rogerian approach. The danger, however, lies in the fallibility of such judgments. Experience and feelings should be considered, but not to the exclusion of many other sources of direction open to the counselor. The growth-counseling concept stresses the utilization of wisdom gained from academic knowledge, research, personal and professional experiences, and impressions gained from a variety of learning experiences. No one source of wisdom for the counselor necessarily carries more weight than another, and he is cautious in making judgments. This should be seen as a case of continuous learning and growing by the counselor in his efforts to continually bolster his capabilities and skills.

   11. Tentativeness and tolerance. Tentativeness in judgments and a tolerance of the client are elements in the relationship, but there are some obvious limitations. Tentativeness is valuable only as it fosters a careful consideration of possible courses of action, and tolerance is of value up to a point. Nothing is to be gained by postponing needed decisions, or by continuing to accept the individual who fails to take constructive action. A careful consideration of the problem and of possible solutions has merit, but caution should be taken against the indecisiveness or a possible impasse. An insistence upon decisions, progress, and observable client growth should characterize the counseling relationship.

   12. The irrationality of behavior. A conclusion as to the irrationality of behavior or thoughts is achieved under the Rogerian approach through insight. The insight then triggers action for improvements. However, the gaining of an insight could be seen as not so much a matter of chance as the result of clever counseling. Its occurrence can be hastened and its value enhanced through counselor intervention and direction. The counselor does not minimize his role but rather views each session as an opportunity to assist the client to learn and to profit from the experience, including the wisdom of the counselor. He does not preach, implore, or impose himself or his thinking upon the client, but he does structure and direct as needed to make the session a fruitful one.

Possible improvements in counseling

Our concern is centered upon the constant betterment of counseling theory and the improvement of techniques. It is the intent of this book to continue to utilize those elements from existing theory that appear to hold the greatest promise, and to develop the techniques that continue to prove most useful.

The client-centered theory with its accompanying techniques has certain strengths. However, it has weaknesses of which the counselor should be aware, and it holds possibilities for improvements.

The lack of direct participation by the counselor and the assumption that the individual will eventually be able to work things out for himself constitute some hazards for many clients. Although it is true that growth comes from active participation and involvement in the therapeutic process, there is a question as to how much responsibility should be assumed by the client. Meaningful and responsible action does not happen just because the counselor thinks it should, but it is rather an outcome of appropriate preparatory experiences. As the individual profits from his experiences and learns to apply what he learns, he is assured of progress toward his goals. A failure to profit from counseling, or any other experience, is also a failure to grow. Essential direction, and in some cases even manipulation by the counselor, are needed to keep a person moving on a course designed to bring results.

Summary

Client-centered counseling had its beginning with Carl R. Rogers. The themes and major concepts of this theory stress the importance of feelings, faith in man, purposefulness of behavior, and client responsibility.

The techniques of the counselor reflect the philosophies underlying the theory, with the reflection of feeling as the principal technique. Careful, attentive listening, with considerable encouragement for an expression of feelings, is another technique.

The core concepts stress the notion that man is basically good, that he has the capacity to solve his problems, and that much of his growth is dependent upon insights. The client is expected to assume considerable responsibility for himself, to eventually see the irrationality of behavior, and to gain therapeutic benefits from the relationship.

Growth counseling accepts in part many of the concepts of this theory, but it sees limitations that should be overcome for more effective counseling. More and firmer participation by the counselor is needed in order to help the individual realize meaningful growth and be adequately prepared to resolve his problems and plan for the future.

Study and discussion problems

1. Identify some conditions or elements from Carl Rogers's background that appear to have a close relationship with some of his theories.
2. Defend the position that this approach may be as much a philosophy as it is a counseling technique.
3. State in a few sentences the crux of the client-centered theory. What are the elements that seem to be the heart of this theory?
4. Develop your own critique of each of the main elements of this theory.

References

Corsini, R., ed. 1973. *Current psychotherapies.* Itasca, Illinois: F. E. Peacock. Pp. 119–165.

Ford, D. H., and Urban, H. B. 1963. *Systems of psychotherapy.* New York: John Wiley and Sons. Pp. 396–444.

Hansen, J. C., Stevic, R. R., and Warner, R. W. 1972. *Counseling: Theory and process.* Boston: Allyn and Bacon. Pp. 75–100.

Patterson, C. H. 1966, 2nd ed., 1973. *Theories of counseling and psychotherapy.* New York: Harper and Row. Pp. 378–413.

Shertzer, B., and Stone, S. C. 1968, 2nd ed., 1974. *Fundamentals of counseling.* Boston: Houghton Mifflin Company. Pp. 214–223.

/ 6 /

Learning theory approaches applied to counseling

The learning theory approaches in counseling and psychotherapy carry this designation because of a utilization of the concepts from learning theory in the field of counseling. Learning theory has been an influence on counseling theory, and the latter has profited from the contributions of learning theory. A number of overlapping theoretical elements are thus involved. Selectivity also plays a part as counseling utilizes only those elements from learning theory that have the greatest practical and utilitarian value.

For example, Patterson (1966) covers six theories all under a main heading of learning theories. It is evident that the coverage in our current writing must be brief and in summary form only. An in-depth coverage should be sought elsewhere.

Some elements of learning theory are used to advantage by the counselor and psychotherapist in formulating appropriate approaches. Since we think of learning as changes in behavior due to conditions other than maturation, the interest of counselors in learning theory becomes understandable. Counseling under these circumstances becomes an application of learning theory.

Background

The background of the learning theory approaches is based essentially upon the following: the reinforcement theory of Dollard and Miller; classical conditioning, with Salter's conditioned reflex therapy as a good example; the reciprocal inhibition of Wolpe; and operant conditioning as proposed by Skinner.

There are other lesser known approaches with some unique elements of their own, and there are approaches that combine and modify elements of the above approaches. Consideration is given here to the four major learning theories as identified above.

Major learning theories

The learning theories have had a great influence upon thought and practice in both instruction and psychotherapy, perhaps to a greater degree than have other theories. This has been useful and desirable as improvements in the teaching-learning situation have been sought, and as counselors and therapists have looked for more effective techniques to utilize in their own work.

Reinforcement theory

Representative of the reinforcement theory is the work of John Dollard and Neal Miller (1950). Unlike the approaches that attempt to apply the principles of conditioning to counseling, this approach attempts to integrate learning theory, the insights of psychoanalysis about human behavior and personality, and the contributions of social science to the social conditions of learning (Patterson 1966). C. L. Hull's behaviorism has been the guide here in the attempt to develop a general science of human behavior. Psychotherapy provides for a look at human mentality, through an application of the laws and theory of learning. Certain fundamental concepts characterize the reinforcement theory.

1. Origin of neurosis. Neurosis is learned through certain kinds of experiences. The neurotic becomes so as he learns patterns of behavior that are inconsistent with his needs and with the expectations of his environment. He continues to develop emotional problems as his behavior results in a failure to deal adequately with his problems. The symptoms of maladjustment, such as phobias, irritability, restlessness, and uncertainty, persist despite any efforts to overcome them. He is capable of performing normally, but he fails to do so because of having learned inappropriate behaviors. Symptoms and repressions are learned and are not the result of instincts or biological conditions.

2. Neurotic behavior. Neurotic behavior occurs and is reinforced as the person reacts to and attempts to adjust to the environment. He persists in the behavior because he has learned to do so, and he doesn't change because of the established pattern in which he has become trapped. His main hope for change rests with his ability to learn new ways of behaving with which he can replace the unwanted behaviors.

A change is difficult, however, because his behavior is the result of a conflict he feels between two or more drives that lead to incompatible responses. He may have difficulty changing his behavior even if he senses and understands the incompatible nature of his responses, but frequently he is not aware of this situation. Change is also difficult because his symptoms actually help to reduce the conflicts, thus resulting in his repeating the behavior.

3. Symptoms and repression. Utilizing a symptom becomes a natural way of behaving for the neurotic, so he continues to behave this way. Repression is also a learned way of behaving, as certain thoughts and considerations are inadvertently subdued and buried in the unconscious.

Classical conditioning

Classical conditioning has a relatively long history; however, the more recent modifications of this theory have greater relevance for counseling and psychotherapy. An example of this is Andrew Salter's "Reflex Therapy" (Patterson 1965). Elements of classical conditioning are thus found in some current counseling approaches.

4. The cause of problems. Personality problems frequently occur as the individual clings to strong inhibitions as a protection against his impulses. The perceived need of the individual to maintain inhibitions in order to make it, or exist in his society, is sometimes exaggerated. This condition then leads to defensive and even neurotic behavior.

The inhibited person tries to give the impression that he is liked and in turn likes others. In reality, his major concern is about himself, and he is not the flexible, congenial person he would like others to think he is. His personal preoccupation contributes to his being a rather tense, anxious, and relatively ineffective individual. His personality characteristics and behavior are essentially fraudulent, as he apologetically tries too hard to please, while still failing to express himself naturally and freely.

5. The influence of conditioning. The individual is conditioned to behave in a particular fashion by the adults in his life and by other environmental influences. The child is subjected to certain pressures toward conformity and pleasing others, resulting in his becoming less spontaneous and natural and more rigid, anxious, and self-critical. As environmental forces are responsible for this conditioning, they must likewise be used to bring about new learning.

6. The development of capacities. The full development of capacities is hindered by fears, anxieties, and apprehensions. The goal of therapy under these circumstances is to help the individual become more relaxed, spontaneous, and productive. Since the diagnosis is always inhibition (Salter 1961), little hope is given for the development and utilization of potentialities and capacities until these inhibitions (Salter 1961) can be reduced or overcome.

Symptoms are dealt with in terms of verbal conditioning, and a knowledge of the past is obtained only for purposes of determining the individual's past conditioning in order to facilitate a reconditioning. The focus of therapy, then, is upon changing behavior, which will then lead to any needed changes in feelings and thoughts. It is through meaningful behavior that capacities are developed and skill improved.

Reciprocal inhibition

This method of psychotherapy dates from about 1944, when Joseph Wolpe, who was serving as a medical military officer, was led to a questioning of traditional psychoanalysis (Patterson 1966). He was attracted to Pavlov, a Russian psychologist, and was apparently fascinated by his work. Later attractions were centered on Clark Hull and his learning theory, and eventually the work of Masserman, Watson, and Rayner in their experiments with neuroses in animals.

This treatment is somewhat restricted to neurotics and to dealing with fears and phobias. It calls for the behavioral manifestation of a response antagonistic to the one selected for extinction. It is the intent of this approach to inhibit or eliminate old responses through the promotion of new responses. Thus, the individual unlearns unwanted responses, learning new ones through reinforcement and repetition.

The crux of this approach is the elicitation of a response antagonistic to anxiety in the presence of anxiety-evoking stimuli accompanied by a complete or partial suppression of the anxiety responses, thus weakening the bond between the stimuli and the anxiety responses (Wolpe 1958).

7. The cause of behavior. Since all behavior is learned, the symptoms of neurotic behavior are also the outcomes of learning. Anxiety is a major cause of neurotic behavior, and anxiety, too, is learned. A person thus becomes neurotic through the persistent expression of symptoms, which he utilizes in an effort to meet needs and to achieve a state of comfort. Inappropriate behavior results from anxieties, which must be reduced or eliminated if behavior is to be changed.

The idea is to replace old responses with new ones in order to achieve more logical behavior. Anxieties are thus replaced by more positive feelings.

8. Neurotic anxiety. Anxiety occurs as an outcome of a threatening situation. The organism reacts according to the envisioned threat of a situation. Neurotic anxiety has been conditioned to intrinsically non-harmful stimuli (Patterson 1966). Putting it more simply, undue anxiety occurs, at a level unwarranted by the circumstances. There are high emotional and biological reactions of such severity as to render the person relatively ineffective. The neurosis that develops is then dealt with by eliminating those responses, which include symptoms of maladjustment, and replacing them with more appropriate responses. Anxiety in this case is the autonomic response patterns that are characteristically part of the organism's response to noxious stimulation (Wolpe 1958).

Operant conditioning

Operant conditioning as developed by B. F. Skinner (1953) is essentially the same as instrumental conditioning and has as its goal a change in behavior. It also has much in common with the other behavior modification approaches, being based upon learning theories.

9. The cause of behavior. Like other behavioristic or behavior modification approaches, operant conditioning assumes that behavior is learned and that it can be unlearned by substituting more desirable behaviors. Unwanted behaviors are eliminated and desired behaviors elicited through reinforcement. This is done by specifying the wanted behavior and then by establishing the appropriate conditions under which wanted behavior is elicited. Positive reinforcement is provided to encourage the wanted behavior, and negative reinforcement is used to discourage unwanted behavior.

10. Programming of behavior. This approach assumes the ability of the therapist and the client to identify the behavior to be changed and to make these needed changes by observing a programmed approach. Attempts are made to eliminate any reinforcement of unwanted behaviors and to develop reinforcements for the wanted behaviors.

This can be achieved by the individual on his own as he learns the technique through therapy. Once the person decides upon a specified behavior, he can set up the conditions for controlling and achieving it.

Behavioral counseling

Behavioral counseling (Krumboltz and Thoresen 1969) is included under the learning theories since it has many elements in common with the approaches identified in this chapter. Its major differences are found in the flexibility of techniques and in a more comprehensive view of the causes of behavior.

11. Psychotherapy as a learning process. The various behaviors are learned as the individual attempts to meet his needs. He persists in those behaviors that appear to bring satisfaction and that result in appropriate reinforcement. Inappropriate behaviors sometimes continue simply because the individual perceives some satisfaction from them or lacks the ability to change. As a lawful and directive process, psychotherapy can be best conducted within a learning theory framework.

12. Variables in psychotherapy. This approach also assumes that the variables in psychotherapy are much the same as those found in other interpersonal situations in which reinforcement, extinction, and acquisition play a part (Carkhuff and Berenson 1967). The counselor is a vital influence in the relationship, as he structures and manipulates the situations for the benefit of efficiency and effectiveness.

13, 14, 15. Essentials in behavior modification. Four major essentials provide an "in-the-nutshell" coverage of this approach (Krumboltz and Thoresen 1969). (1) A counseling goal is formulated. The client is helped to establish a goal that is acceptable to him and that is subject to evaluation. (2) The techniques used are varied and modified to fit the client. (3) Experimentation is used freely with a broad area of approaches. (4) Procedures are constantly improved upon as relevant evidence becomes available. Self-correction, feedback, evaluation, and research are all used to improve counseling.

16, 17, 18. Strategies of behavior modification. The strategies of this approach are focused upon the ultimate purpose of all counseling, and that is to change behavior. Since undesirable behavior is a product of learning, so, too, may desirable behavior be learned. The unlearning and the learning needed to bring about behavioral changes are achieved through a variety of therapeutic approaches. The application of reinforcement to achieve appropriate behavior, and of no reinforcement to bring about the extinction of unwanted behaviors, is the focus of therapeutic attention.

Techniques and tools of learning theories

The techniques of the learning theories (behavior modification) are very similar. The few distinctions do not justify a clear separation of them. Reinforcement for fixing and habituating desired behavior and extinction procedures for eliminating undesired behaviors characterize these techniques. Therapeutic emphasis is upon structure that will result in the individual's behaving in a desired fashion and in the abandonment of unwanted behaviors.

Reinforcement theory of Dollard and Miller

Some of the techniques of this approach are similar to those used in the psychoanalytic approach, but with some differences in emphasis. A talking out of the client's concerns is encouraged, and free association is used to reduce tensions and anxieties. Verbal or other kinds of rewards or reinforcement are used to encourage talking in order to get at repressed thoughts or events. This reinforcement is provided for through the counselor's attitude of acceptance and understanding, and through his sincere attention.

Transference is used as a source of information for the counselor. It, along with free association, permits a freedom of expression, which identifies emotional elements that may require careful attention. The counselor or therapist helps the individual to identify the emotional responses by labeling or naming the response. This action, then, serves as the instrument by which the client is able to deal with the concerns, or the responses they represent, through higher mental processes.

The therapist focuses on eliminating anxiety or fear responses. Thoughts and verbal responses are modified, and the therapist encourages the transfer of this new relationship developed in therapy to the real world. This is done by pointing out and by helping the individual experience the rewards that come from behavior changes. These techniques give objectivity to the relationship, and their value becomes evident as the client makes significant behavior changes.

Salter's classical conditioning

Since this theory places considerable emphasis upon inhibition as a cause of all psychological problems (Salter 1961), the focus of treatment is upon the removal of inhibitions through reconditioning. This provides for a full emotional release through a verbal expression of emotions, which leads to needed changes in behavior.

An increase in excitation is essential to overcoming inhibitions and bettering behavior. Certain techniques for increasing excitation are thus used and include the following: (1) Free talk is an open, unrestrained expression of deepest feelings and includes appropriate gestures and facial expressions. (2) Verbal expressions emphasize aggression and a conscious and deliberate reference to oneself and one's importance. (3) Expressions of agreement with praise received are manifested clearly and unabashedly.

The techniques are quite direct and are designed to encourage many kinds of expressions through which the individual's sensitivities may be reduced. New emotional habits are thus developed to replace old habits. This is accomplished through suggestion, persuasion, advice, logic, and even command. The idea is to overcome the strong inhibiting feelings and behaviors that characteristically control and render the individual ineffective.

Wolpe's reciprocal inhibition

There are some rather clear-cut procedures under this therapeutic approach, all of which are designed to overcome phobias or fears and unproductive behavior. More effective behavior is the goal. The therapeutic value of empathy, an attitude of concern and positive regard, as demonstrated by the counselor, is open to question in this approach. Greater credence is given to techniques that will move the client toward new behaviors.

Therapy begins with a detailed clinical history, for purposes of identifying the historical antecedents that have determined the neurotic reactions. The history includes family relationships, education, sex life, and important social relationships.

The tools used include the Willoughby Personality Schedule, the Bernreuter Self-Sufficiency Scale, and a Fear Inventory Schedule. A medical examination is required if there is the possibility of organic disease having a part in the individual's problem. Data from these instruments are then utilized in determining the most appropriate treatment methods.

The therapeutic methods include assertive training, sexual arousal for the treatment of impotence and frigidity, relaxation, and hypnosis. Systematic desensitization is the most frequently used system for overcoming fears and phobias.

Skinner's operant conditioning

Since behavior change is the objective here, conditioning techniques are employed to elicit or shape the desired behavior. The goal behavior is established and reinforcement in rewards or positive feedback is given with each correct behavior. The desired behavior then becomes habitual and further reinforcement is unnecessary. The non-reinforcement of undesired behaviors, and in some cases the application of punishment, are used to bring about extinction.

A programming of behavior is also done as the individual decides upon the behavior to be followed, and as he systematically avoids any unwanted behaviors. Structure, persuasion, reinforcement, modeling and programming all have important places in this system.

Krumboltz's behavior modification

Flexibility characterizes the techniques of this approach. The idea is to use whatever techniques seem to have the greatest merit for helping a particular individual. There is immediate focus upon a goal. The individual is expected to have something in mind that he expects to achieve.

Positive reinforcement is used, but as a part of a positive work-relationship with the client. Other techniques include modeling, role playing, cognitive structuring, simulation, confrontation and counter-conditioning. These are normally used in conjunction with each other, with no effort to follow just one technique (Krumboltz and Thoresen 1969).

Responses to the learning theories

The attempts to criticize these theories are characterized by considerable agreement and by a concern for overcoming the existing limitations of these approaches. We might, for example, take the position that one major theory should serve as a guide in all counseling and psychotherapy. And, although this position has merit, it also has some definite limitations, the most pronounced or obvious of which is that no one theory is this popular or influential. So, in criticizing these theories, we purposely identify their limitations and provide some suggestions for possible improvements.

Reinforcement theory

1. Origin of neurosis. The origin of neurosis may indeed be found in one's experiences, but growth counseling has an answer to this through preventive measures. Krumboltz likewise strongly supports this position, as do others who have given prevention somewhat less attention. The counselor and teacher are alert, under this system, to any possible sign of developing maladjustments. Efforts are continuously made to help each child find satisfactory outlets for his emotions and learn behavior suitable to his needs. In addition to preventive measures, any needed corrective action is taken early, and any possible tendency to reinforce an inappropriate behavior is avoided. Early corrective action is thus an essential aspect of prevention, as it quickly directs the child's thoughts and actions toward attractive, suitable behaviors. And since it is most difficult to change well-established habit patterns, steps are taken to avoid such occurrences.

2. Neurotic behavior. Since neurotic behavior does occur and is reinforced as the individual attempts to adjust to the environment, growth counseling concentrates upon the immediate elimination of any possible reinforcement of neurotic behavior. Explanations are made to the individual as to the reasons for the inappropriateness of the behavior, and he is encouraged to express himself concerning his feelings and thoughts related to the behavior.

The counselor takes the initiative in structuring the environment in order to create a desirable situation and to avoid unwanted conditions. Considerable emphasis is given to providing appropriate reinforcement for agreed-upon, desired behavior.

3. *Symptoms and repression.* Symptoms and repressions need not become habitual behaviors if appropriate precautions are taken. Direct efforts are provided by the counselor in helping the individual recognize and replace symptoms with more appropriate adjustment mechanisms. The person is taught to recognize a symptom, ascertain its possible causes, and then decide on a course of action. Emphasis is given to a candid discussion of what the client feels may be blocking his progress to new insights and to better behavior.

It is assumed that repressions are less likely to occur as the individual finds satisfactions in his associations with others and as he takes greater pride in his own achievements. The point here is that he is helped in the development of greater inner strength, which makes possible a better relationship with others, thus reducing the need for questionable behavioral outlets.

Classical conditioning

4. *The cause of problems.* Considerable credence is given to Salter's notion that inhibitions are at the root of many personality problems. However, these are problems associated with character disorders, sociopathic behavior, and others that have little or no relationship with inhibitions. Salter stresses this belief, and it appears to have merit as an explanation for some behaviors. The tensions and apprehensions endured by many people have their origin in unrealistic demands upon self and in an overwhelming compulsion to please others. The inclination each individual has for free expression and action sometimes encounters censure, which frequently causes the individual to become very self-conscious and fearful. The self-confidence prompted by the growth-counseling concept provides considerable protection against unrealistic inhibitions. The individual is taught to express himself naturally and freely and to practice behaviors that provide for the maximum of expression. There is an avoidance of energy dissipation in needless controls or

worry, as the individual learns how to utilize his emotions advantageously.

The individual learns, through appropriate controls and direction, how to love others with an assurance that others will also care about him. These skills and attitudes come as a result of the knowledge he has gained about the avenues of self-expression open to him. Undue restraints are neither environmentally nor self-imposed since he has learned to find satisfaction in relatively uninhibited expressions. Appropriate controls are utilized as augmentors, but never as inhibitors, to free, wholesome behaviors.

5. The influence of conditioning. If the individual is conditioned to behave in a particular fashion by the adults around him and the environment in which he finds himself, then the implications for counseling are clear. A conditioning in the direction of desired behaviors should be practiced.

Counseling, then, provides for a correct use of adult and environmental forces in changing behavior and in structuring for desirable behavior. Instead of classical conditioning being the heart of change, the nature of the counseling relationship triggers the change. All so-called "conditioning" is thus positive, and a chain reaction of desirable behavior is thus triggered, with the reinforcement coming from the success of the individual's behavior.

6. The development of capacities. Fears, anxieties, and apprehensions do, indeed, inhibit the development of one's capacities. Since growth counseling stresses the development of capacities as the heart of its approach, expedient action is taken to avoid any condition that may prove thwarting to this goal. Counseling procedures include reflection of feeling, verbal feedback of the emotional and intellectual expressions, explanations as to possible causes of difficulties, exploration of alternatives, and a commitment to a course of action. The individual is thus helped to identify and have confidence in his strengths and in his ability to deal with any occurring situation. Logic, reason, and thought are utilized in making an accurate perception of the environment. The counselor discourages wasting time on relatively inconsequential matters, or upon conditions that are unalterable, and continuously stresses productive spontaneous action. The fears and anxieties of the individual are not ignored, but they are dealt with indirectly through confidence-bolstering experiences provided for through counseling.

Reciprocal inhibition

7. The cause of behavior. Closely allied with the above points is Wolpe's contention that anxiety is a cause of neurotic behavior and that all behavior is learned. Growth counseling seeks to reduce anxieties through the development of new thought and behavioral patterns, a position also taken by Dollard and Miller. So, instead of attempting to deal with the behaviors triggered by undue anxieties, appropriate preventive measures are taken. If anxieties do occur, then the course of therapy is toward building up the individual through suggestions, home assignments, positive reinforcement for successes, and through preparing for anxiety-evoking experiences. The possibly fatalistic attitude of conventional treatment is avoided, as a more positive attitude toward the individual and his abilities is fostered.

For example, a moving train will kill or maim anyone who places himself upon the tracks. Since anxiety may be just as devastating to the personality as the train is to the physical being, the avoidance of such a catastrophe is the logical solution. Or if it does occur despite precautions, immediate remedial action is taken. Just as one can normally avoid a confrontation with a train, so too may he avoid a showdown with an intense anxiety. He is also helped in choosing and adapting certain procedures designed to reduce anxiety or minimize its possible effects.

8. Neurotic anxiety. Anxiety is, indeed, frequently the outcome in the face of a threatening event. As the organism reacts to the threat of this event, the symptoms of anxiety appear. And we have learned under reciprocal inhibition that it is possible to replace the old responses, such as those evoked by a threatening situation, with new responses. Of even greater importance under growth counseling is the concept and a system that foster a continuous development of many positive behaviors, which lead to more productive and rewarding outcomes. In this case the energies expended provide results in added achievements. There is resistance, then, to the idea that time and energy must be expended in breaking old habits in order to develop new ones. Growth counseling fosters the idea that an action should be on the positive side and that unwanted habits can be eliminated simply by concentrating upon the development of wanted habits and behaviors.

The fact that avoidance, or aversive, conditioning plays an important part in reciprocal inhibition suggests the importance of recognizing its merits. Although some theorists regard punishment as intolerable, or at least unproductive, the fact remains that avoidance conditioning is effective in extinguishing undesired behaviors. The most valid complaint against this system appears to be that if avoidance conditioning is not coupled with a positively reinforced new behavior its effect may lack permanence. An example may be found in the relatively high recidivism rate found in the penal system. The reason may be that no alternative, positively reinforced behavior is provided the inmate.

Operant conditioning

9. The cause of behavior. A change in behavior must always be a goal of education and of counseling. However, the change we emphasize in counseling is one of constant progress in both attitude and behavior changes and of building upon that which has already been achieved. This has little to do with breaking old habits, since it is the intent that they never develop in the first place. Of course, this aim is an ideal, and it is impossible to suggest that bad habits will never develop. They will occur even under the most favorable of circumstances. However, little is to be gained by more than a casual reference to unwanted behaviors. Hopefully, these will be eliminated incidentally through a concentration upon desirable, positive behaviors.

The system for eliminating unwanted behaviors includes providing for a wide variety of wholesome, appealing activities, which by their nature and appeal are so attractive that there is little inclination for inappropriate behavior. The attack is subtle and indirect, but no less potent. Instead of stating or implying, "Tommy, you have been stealing and we must break you of this habit," the focus is upon the development of positive behaviors that will naturally and logically prevail with a gradual elimination of the old habit.

10. Programming of behavior. The practice of obtaining the desired behaviors through reinforcement has its merits, but some definite limitations. The failure to reinforce as a device for eliminating unwanted behavior may also be at least partially wishful thinking. Appropriate feedback, allowing the behaver to know how his behavior is being received by others, is desirable. But the possible overdependence of the individual upon some reinforcing elements may be a deterrent rather than a stimulant to his progress and growth. A failure to reinforce unwanted behavior, likewise, is no guarantee that the behavior will not persist. Needs must be identified and efforts made to meet those needs. If this is not done, the individual will persist in behavior that relieves tension and holds some promise for fulfillment. The fact that his choice of behavior is erroneous does not alter the nature of the situation.

The possibly mechanistic connotation inevitably implied in the use of reinforcement to obtain desired behavior is distasteful to growth counseling. Since considerable credit is given to the individual's sense of pride and his personal integrity, he has a major responsibility for helping in the selection of behavior and in the skills to be developed. The reinforcement comes from the personal satisfaction and sense of pride he experiences from having achieved an objective or having followed a plan through to its conclusion. True, satisfying, permanent growth occurs by virtue of engaging in stimulating, exciting, satisfying experiences, not from reinforcements that may have only a remote relationship to the person's real interests and aspirations. The counselor strives to influence this growth through personal encouragement and environmental modification. However, the individual himself is the key to his own successes and to his own sense of pride and personal satisfaction.

Behavioral counseling

11. Psychotherapy as a learning process. Psychotherapy should certainly be a learning process from which the individual may learn and practice new behaviors. It is a case of determining what he is to learn and how permanently useful it is to be. A principal contention of growth counseling is that the contact between counselor and client and the relationship developed hold essential growth-promoting possibilities. This implies counselor competence and efficiency in the utilization of the counseling time. The counselor's sensitivity to the client, and his awareness of the learning possibilities, make the experience a most fruitful one.

Counseling is thus characterized by appropriate planning and by an intelligent use of time and of available resources. The counselor is keenly aware of the client's needs and observant as to his capacities by which needs may be met and successes realized.

12. Reinforcement, extinction, and acquisition. These are major elements in behavior modification, but they have only a minor role in growth counseling. There is a realization that appropriate forms of reinforcement have a part in learning correct behavior, that some extinction is essential to progress, and that the acquisition of needed skills and attitudes will facilitate development. However, the emphasis is more logically given to those techniques that contribute directly to growth and that promote the personal responsibility of the individual. The feeling of satisfaction gained from having given a task or an idea one's best efforts is sufficient reinforcement for the repetition of the behavior that triggered the satisfaction. And the disappointment endured from a failure to achieve, or to have done one's best, is frequently sufficiently discouraging to eliminate any repetition of the behavior.

In growth counseling the emphasis is upon the development of internal strengths through rewarding, self-satisfying experiences, rather than upon an externally imposed reward system. Through deliberate efforts to do a task well, the individual learns to depend upon himself for his successes. He learns the importance of self-initiative and self-discipline, and he recognizes the need for the proper channeling of his efforts in order to achieve his goals. As he concentrates upon engaging in only logical and acceptable behavior, inappropriate behaviors occur less frequently, and they are generally amenable to immediate correction.

The acquisition of knowledge, skills, and attitudes is taking place constantly under this system. However, these acquisitions occur more incidentally and as outcomes of other behaviors, rather than as a direct result of a specified plan. The individual thus has a variety of experiences in a broad framework of possibilities, all of which emphasize action and involvement leading to personal growth and satisfaction.

13. Goals. The value of having a goal, toward which the client is to work, is determined by the degree to which this procedure contributes to the personal growth of the individual. The limitations of having a precise goal frequently include the notion that this goal represents an end in itself. Once the goal is achieved, the individual may feel that there is no need for further action. Growth counseling subscribes to the concept of having a goal, but with the added notion that the goal must have a direct relationship to the growth process of the individual. The attainment of individual goals, then, has merit if such an attainment constitutes a step toward broader, deeper, more comprehensive and more permanent achievements. Any connotation of narrowness is avoided in following this goal-oriented technique.

The relative simplicity of achieving a particular and limited goal can be misleading to the individual. His attitude could be, "Now I have achieved a goal; I have arrived." In reality, any one goal constitutes no more than a small fraction of what the person is capable of achieving. It is this capacity for sensational growth and progress of which he should be constantly aware. To be satisfied with rather minor achievements based upon specified goals well below the capability level of the individual would be unfortunate. There is indeed, however, much to be said for the carefully delineated reinforcement schedules utilized in behavior modification approaches. The successful application of this technique serves to support its use. Growth counseling provides for the internalization of an insight and for its proper application. This minimizes the possibilities of an overdependence upon limiting one's efforts to a specified goal and of not performing at a level commensurate with one's capabilities.

14. Variability. The concept of variability in technique utilization for goal achievement has considerable merit. Flexibility in the selection and use of techniques permits a better accommodation of the client, and it may also increase the effectiveness of the counselor. This position assumes, however, that the counselor is knowledgeable on the theories and practices of counseling, and thus capable of using the techniques selected with expedience and effectiveness.

15. Research. Research is encouraged by the very nature of growth counseling, and significant findings are utilized in bettering counseling. However, considerable emphasis is given to personal observations and impressions gained by the counselor in his experiences. The awareness and sensitivity of the counselor are stressed as prerequisites to the creation of an atmosphere from which significant improvements may be made.

16. Change. A change in behavior is essential in personal growth and is an objective in growth counseling. This assumes, however, an intelligent use of psychological energies and of environmental resources. Behavior change, then, is incidental to a growth in depth, through which appropriate decisions may be made in keeping with new insights and with more ambitious aspirations.

17. Reinforcement. Although it is possible to initiate desired behaviors in the individual through immediate reinforcement, growth counseling depends more upon the will, character, and integrity of the individual. There is a greater freedom of choice here, increasing, perhaps, the possibilities for error, but at the same time bettering the individual's chances for gaining insights and reaching certain conclusions with unlimited and permanent value. Appropriate behavior may be learned with no more reinforcement than the feeling of satisfaction that accompanies a worthy achievement. The feelings of dissatisfaction and disappointment in oneself, likewise, tend to eliminate the improper or fruitless behaviors.

18. Behavior extinction. Behavior extinction is obviously essential to improvement and to more effective living. It is achieved, however, in growth counseling under a somewhat different philosophy than that which advocates the removal of reinforcers. The avoidance of inappropriate behavior is achieved to a degree through the emphasis given to positive behaviors. The individual is so involved in practicing behaviors previously identified as promising that there is little inclination to experiment with behaviors of questionable value. The maturity, intelligence, resourcefulness, and capacity of the individual are all stressed as initiators of desirable conduct. To conduct oneself inappropriately under this system would be a breach of confidence in oneself. The individual understands and accepts the responsibility to behave rationally. He does not resist reinforcement when his behavior pleases himself and others, nor does he become concerned over the absence of reinforcement when extinction is required. His real concern rests with his own sense of pride and integrity. He feels capable of eliminating undesirable behavior, just as he possesses the confidence to adopt and practice appropriate behavior.

Summary

Many concepts from learning theory have been utilized in counseling and psychotherapy and have contributed markedly to the quality of these professional services.

The principal theories include the reinforcement theory of Dollard and Miller; classical conditioning, which includes the reflex therapy of Salter; the reciprocal inhibition of Wolpe; the operant conditioning of Skinner; and the behavioral counseling of Krumboltz.

The core elements of these theories focus upon the notion that neurotic or maladaptive behavior is learned through habitual repetition and reinforcement. A change in behavior thus becomes necessary and is achieved through reinforcing desired behaviors and failing to reinforce unwanted behaviors.

Personality problems are frequently caused by strong inhibitions developed as a protection against strong impulses. Anxiety may also be a cause of maladjustment, thus calling for a replacement of old responses with new ones.

Behavior change is the constant goal of therapy and is achieved through reinforcement.

Growth counseling accepts many of the concepts of these theories, but it places less emphasis upon reinforcement as a means for changing behavior. The satisfaction gained from serious efforts to do well serves as the reinforcer of desired behavior, and the personal growth achieved by the individual provides the necessary internal strength for appropriate behavior changes and constant growth.

Study and discussion problems

1. Identify what you regard as the most significant contributions of learning theory to counseling theory.
2. Briefly outline the main points from each of the following:
   a. Reinforcement theory;
   b. Classical conditioning;
   c. Reciprocal inhibition;
   d. Operant conditioning;
   e. Behavioral counseling or behavior modification.
3. Review the principal devices or techniques utilized in the above approaches.
4. Develop your own critique of any or all of the theories listed under problem 2.

References

Corsini, R., ed. 1973. *Current psychotherapies.* Itasca, Illinois: F. E. Peacock. Pp. 207–249.

Ford, D. H., and Urban, H. B. 1963. *Systems of psychotherapy.* New York: John Wiley and Sons. Pp. 211–303.

Hansen, J. C., Stevic, R. R., and Warner, R. W. 1972. *Counseling: Theory and process.* Boston: Allyn and Bacon. Pp. 101–138.

Patterson, C. H. 1966, 2nd ed., 1973. *Theories of counseling and psychotherapy.* New York: Harper and Row. Pp. 79–211.

Shertzer, B., and Stone, S. C. 1968, 2nd ed., 1974. *Fundamentals of counseling.* Boston: Houghton Mifflin Company. Pp. 194–202.

Wolpe, J. 1969. *The practice of behavior therapy.* New York: Pergamon Press.

/ 7 /

The trait-factor approach

The trait-factor approach has served as a guide for counselors in various educational and clinical settings for many years. It has constituted something of a contrast to the client-centered approach in a number of its fundamental precepts. For example, it emphasizes direct involvement of the counselor and gives him considerable responsibility for the decisions made. It also stresses his role as a vital one in directing the individual toward appropriate vocational and educational choices.

It also stresses the intellectual aspects of decision making and problem resolution, in contrast to the client-centered approach, which stresses the emotional elements of a problem. Where client-centered counseling focuses upon the client as the source of decision making, the trait-factor approach sees the counselor as the focus of the needed guidance and direction toward appropriate decisions.

Background

This approach has its origin with Frank Parsons in Boston during the very early 1900s. He saw the need for counseling as a source of assistance to young people in making job choices. His work served as a pioneering effort for many who have since followed his lead.

The University of Minnesota is regarded as the focal institution for the promulgation of this approach; however, that institution's contributions have certainly not been limited to this one theory.

Walter Bingham, John Darley, Donald G. Paterson, and E. G. Williamson have been the major contributors of thought to this approach. The latter has made contributions to the counseling field beyond the limitations of one approach, however, thus justifying a separate section on Williamson and the Minnesota point of view in this chapter.

Major theoretical elements

Like any other theory or approach in counseling and psychotherapy, the trait-factor approach has certain distinguishing elements. It also has a number of elements common to other approaches. This condition makes for a strengthening of all counseling theory, as the various approaches supplement each other.

Concepts underlying the trait-factor approach

This theory focuses upon the concept of evaluation or measurement as a device for assessing an individual's traits and characteristics. Data gained are then used in helping the individual toward appropriate vocational choices. Considerably less attention is given to personal feelings and to behavior changes than is the case with other theories. The idea is one of assessing traits and of then making plans for the future on the basis of the traits.

1. *The assessment of traits.* The core of this approach is that man has certain measurable traits, the assessment of which serves as a guide in matching an individual with the demands of a particular vocation or profession. A basic requirement is one of providing suitable instruments for the measurement of these traits, as well as establishing procedures

for gaining considerable information about the requirements of many jobs and vocations.

2. *The individual and his environment.* The individual constitutes sources of information about himself that can be used in decision making and in plan formulation. The environment in which the individual finds himself is also a rich source of information critical to the making of appropriate decisions. It is not the intent of this theory to make any great changes in either, but rather to utilize them as they are.

For example, assessments of the individual reveal certain qualities and characteristics, and observations of the environment likewise identify its strengths and limitations. Appropriate decisions are made on the basis of the information gained.

3. *A synthesis of data.* An important step in this approach is a synthesis of data gained from a number of sources into a meaningful pattern of information. This information is then fully utilized by the counselor and the client in identifying and resolving existing problems, and in making appropriate plans for immediate and future action. Judgments and decisions are made on the basis of information at hand, and to some extent upon the wisdom of the counselor. Data about the person are combined with facts about the environment, such as job requirements and opportunities, in helping the individual make decisions.

4. *Predictions about successes.* Predictions as to one's chances for success in various educational and vocational choices are possible. Such predictions are based upon accumulated data about the person and about the choices open to him. Objectivity, sound judgment, and experience underlie all decisions, and the appropriateness of decisions can be readily ascertained by virtue of the information accumulated.

5. *Handling emotional problems.* Emotional problems, such as anxiety, have their origin in the individual's inability to make decisions and are handled accordingly. In other words, little direct attention is given to the emotions, but rather the focus is upon the decision-making process. It is believed that if the individual can make, observe, and follow through on certain decisions his anxieties, or other emotional problems,

will dissipate. The emotionality has its source in uncertainty, indecision, and lack of information. Once the uncertainty is overcome, through making a decision based upon information at hand, there is no longer an emotional problem.

6. *The availability of instruments.* The success of this approach depends markedly upon the availability of proper measuring instruments and upon information about educational and vocational opportunities. This also suggests the need for competent personnel to interpret the data to the client. Stress is thus given to the quality and appropriateness of the instruments and to the information about educational and vocational opportunities.

Techniques of counseling

In deciding upon techniques to be used, the counselor assumes considerable responsibility. However, the client still has much to say about choices, as efforts are made to expand the range of choice possibilities (Williamson 1965). The techniques to be used under this system are relatively easy to anticipate once the concepts of the theory are understood. The techniques are quite precise, data-oriented, objective, and logical, and are in keeping with a knowledge of the client and information about the possible choices open to him. The task of the counselor, then, is one of aiding the individual toward a better understanding of himself and toward self-management through the assessment of assets and liabilities in keeping with his goals (Williamson 1965).

Interpretation is used in helping the client understand and use the results of measuring instruments. Advice giving is used, but within a setting of objectivity and with client participation. Bibliotherapy and study assignments have a place, as the client is expected to increase his knowledge about himself, others, and his environment.

Informal discussions, group counseling, field trips, work experiences, role playing, and many other techniques are used to promote the making of wise decisions. Variety thus characterizes the approaches used, since counseling is dedicated to the cultivation and development of human potentialities.

A critique of the trait-factor approach

Logic, objectivity, planning, and meaningful action characterize this approach. And since its background is found in vocational counseling, it has had a long and interesting history.

A response to this approach

The possible merits of this approach are fairly obvious, and they are emphasized by counselors who are comfortable with a rather directive approach, that stresses assessment and decision making on the basis of available data.

1. The assessment of traits. The assessment of traits has value, but it also has some definite limitations, necessitating our taking the view that this is an oversimplification and that assessment is only a preliminary step to a sound helping relationship. The measurement of traits, then, is only remotely related to the focus of growth counseling, which is one of capitalizing upon and improving one's capacities and capabilities. Although it is true that each individual is unique, he also has many commonalities that are utilized in helping all individuals toward full development. In other words, the uniqueness or commonality of the individual is only incidental to this concept of maximum development. Assessment has a place, then, only to the degree to which the information gained has immediate utilitarian value to the individual. Information gained serves merely as a means to an end, and exact scores as measuring instruments should not be given undue credence. Growth counseling is more interested in approximations on traits measured, and even more specifically upon the implications that any data may have for the individual.

2. The individual and his environment. The individual and his environment do constitute sources of information, but this information is regarded by growth counseling as only a minor and a beginning point. Plans and decisions are made in growth counseling on the basis of anticipated growth, aspirations, and ambitious expectations. The idea is to encourage each person to aim high and strive diligently toward appropriate and realistic goals. The element of optimism and yearning characterized here provides the impetus for unusually high and worthy achievements.

3. A synthesis of data. A synthesis and utilization of data has considerable value in counseling, as these procedures lend structure and objectivity to counseling. However, how much these procedures are helpful in building self-confidence, and in bolstering self-esteem, is open to question. The mere sharing of data with a student may have no value, and might constitute a threat to the individual who already is lacking in self-confidence. Any data gained under the growth-counseling concept are used to develop and bolster self-esteem. This obviously calls for techniques beyond the interpretation of data. The sense of dignity and of importance is constantly protected and supported by the counselor. Threats of any kind are avoided, and the positive elements of the situation are stressed. The decisions made are based upon a combination of conditions, including personal needs, character traits, goals and aspirations, motivation and current facts.

4. Predictions about successes. The prediction of successes is of questionable value in growth counseling. Since the emphasis is upon personal growth, including the development of personality traits and needed skills, success becomes a key point. Too, as genuine progress is made in personal achievements, the individual's success, no matter how it is defined, becomes assured. A "success" today thus provides the encouragement for action and the groundwork for additional achievements. The value of any possible prediction is determined by its influence in stimulating an individual to do his best and by its worth in providing some structure for a course of action.

5. Handling emotional problems. Emotional problems of some types may have their origin in one's inability to make decisions. However, the ability to make decisions does not necessarily insulate one against emotional difficulties. In fact, the arbitrary making of decisions may well trigger situations that will evoke anxieties and other emotional situations.

In growth counseling, one goal is to avoid emotional problems through the stressing of personality development, and in the constant improvement of behavior. Any tendency toward indecisiveness is thus replaced by positive action as the individual learns to look to himself for the needed strength, and as he capitalizes upon the wisdom of the counselor. The solution to emotional problems thus rests with the competence and confidence of the individual and with his developing abilities to utilize all of the positive elements within his environment.

6. *The availability of instruments*. The availability of measuring instruments is critical to the trait-factor approach, thus placing some limitations on the counseling relationship. Too much dependence upon recorded data could result in a minimization of the importance of the individual as a human being. Instruments of assessment have a place in growth counseling only to the degree to which they provide information that is readily translated into incentives and encouragement for a more intensive pursuit of goals. Data observed in relative isolation have only limited value. It is what these data do to and for the individual and the degree to which they prompt meaningful action that determine their ultimate worth.

Williamson and the Minnesota point of view

Most of what has been said in the discussion of the trait-factor approach also applies to Williamson and the Minnesota point of view. However, there are some additional, although related, elements that justify separate consideration.

The philosophies and concepts of this approach are based on the logical and the rational (Patterson 1966), and counseling is closely allied with education as a form of instruction. One goal of education is that of helping each individual realize his full potential (Williamson 1950). Counseling under this philosophy is thus much broader than psychotherapy, as it focuses on the total welfare of the individual. "Personalism" is the term given to this concept of counseling.

Concepts underlying this approach

A focus of this approach embraces the notion that the student should not be left to his own limited devices for gaining the most from his educational experiences. He should, in other words, be persuaded and even prodded a little to make the most of himself and his educational opportunities. Since the student has had only limited experiences, and is relatively uninformed, he can profit from the wisdom and judgment of the counselor.

1. Counseling and instruction interrelated. In an instructional setting, the student is taught, directed, and guided. Much of what occurs in counseling is likewise of an instructional nature. The client is given information, and its possible use is identified. Explanations are made to the student as guidelines for a possible course of action.

2. A realization of potential. The educational effort is directed toward helping each person realize his greatest potential. Some impatience may characterize the counselor as he thoughtfully and meaningfully attempts to direct the individual toward important goals.

3. Rationality and capability of client. The counselor assumes that the individual has capabilities and that he is logical and rational in his thinking. The client thus has considerable responsibility for plans and for decision making.

4. Self-actualization through counselor assistance. Since self-actualization and high attainments are regarded as the client's principal goals, it is the counselor's function to help him achieve these goals. The effort calls for considerable commitment from the client and for an active involvement by the counselor.

5. Behavior changes. Changes in behavior are realized as the individual sees the need for them in terms of his goals and his increasing self-understanding. And since counseling is essentially a teaching relationship (Patterson 1966), it is the function of the counselor to help the student toward better self-understanding and to direct him in needed behavior changes.

6. Individual freedom. The freedom of the individual in decision and plan making is respected, and he is expected to be deeply involved in all aspects of counseling. He is also expected to give considerable effort to problem resolution while on his own. The counselor does, however, make his influence felt, and he gives the client the benefit of his knowledge and experience.

Individual excellence, or "arette," is seen as a value commitment by each client (Williamson 1967). This philosophy avoids an overemphasis upon techniques in counseling to the exclusion of appropriate attention to the quality of the individual's life, and to his excellence as a human being.

Counseling techniques

Although the philosophical elements of this approach are brought to bear, the techniques used are characterized by breadth and flexibility. A careful consideration is accorded the humane aspects of counseling in which the needs, wants, and aspirations of the client are given careful consideration.

The five steps of analysis, synthesis, diagnosis, counseling, and follow-up (Williamson 1965) are used as guidelines. Their use suggests an objective and scientific approach, but not an abandonment of flexibility or warmth. The five categories of techniques include: (1) forcing conformity, (2) changing the environment, (3) selecting the appropriate environment, (4) learning needed skills, and (5) changing attitudes (Patterson 1965; Williamson 1950). The techniques are then implemented through the: (1) establishment of rapport, (2) cultivation of self-understanding, (3) planning of a program of action, (4) carrying out of a plan, and (5) referral to other personnel workers.

Advice, suggestions, recommendations, persuasion, and listening are all techniques of this approach. Each is used as needed, or in conjunction with other acceptable techniques.

A critique of the Minnesota point of view

Many of the concepts proposed under this approach are acceptable to growth counseling, but there are some differences in terms of interpretation and in degree of emphasis. Explanations of these differences follow.

1. Counseling and instruction interrelated. Counseling is, for example, a form of instruction, but not in the same sense as is classroom instruction. The client gains information in counseling that is helpful to him in making decisions and in increasing his self-understanding. The client is in a sense a learner, but not in the same theoretical structure as a learner in the classroom. In counseling, he is a very active participant in a sharing relationship, so the learning that occurs is somewhat incidental to the total process of personal development.

We may then conclude that the realization of such goals as continuing self-actualization and self-fulfillment is facilitated through the attainment and utilization of information gained through counseling. More important, however, are the stimulation and encouragement the individual receives in counseling. Herein lies the real value of counseling no matter what theory embraces it. A merit of growth counseling is its commitment to go beyond the known, the simple, and the obvious. Depth of understanding is a constant goal.

2. A realization of potential. The realization of one's full potential should of course be a major goal of all forms of counseling. This is, as Williamson suggests, a responsibility of all of education. How well this responsibility is met is, however, a serious question, and growth counseling provides more precise possibilities for a realization of this responsibility through its well-structured approaches. Less is left to chance than is true with the conventional counseling approaches. A well-organized counseling program aims to help each person to a higher level of achievement and fulfillment through "encouragement," counseling, and a drastic improvement in the learning environment. Within this structure, the counselor's efforts are directed toward helping each individual sense the thrilling possibilities open to him. Growth counseling does not accept or settle for mediocrity in thought or actions, or for the average that normally satisfies society and the school.

3. Rationality and capability of client. The assumption that the client is rational and capable and therefore able to help himself obviously has merit. However, this assumption does not presume the presence of equally important character and personality attributes such as attitude, ambition, integrity, desire, and commitment. Growth counseling both taps and assists in developing any and all traits regarded as essential to the individual's continuing progress and welfare.

4. Self-actualization through counselor assistance. Self-actualization through high attainments and enriched living should be the goals of all counseling. However, there are degrees of fulfillment and achievement, and it is only with a superior performance and relatively high achievements that growth counseling is satisfied. The individual is prompted to be discontent with mediocrity and to seek the satisfactions to come from superior efforts and worthy attainments. The attitude of relative content experienced by many individuals is replaced by a serious desire to make the most of one's potentialities. Self-actualization is thus seen as an ongoing process with never-ending possibilities for improvements.

Under this system, an achievement is viewed as worthy only if it is beyond a point of normal expectations, and if each successive achievement surpasses the last one. Each success and activity thus provides the experience and the motivation for the next more challenging task. Growth is thus a continuing process with no end in sight.

5. Behavior changes. Behavior change is recognized as an essential to better adjustment by all major theories; however, the amount of emphasis given to the concept varies somewhat. Changes in behavior are seen in growth counseling as natural outcomes of the insights and the increasing maturity of the individual. Modifications in behavior are thus constantly taking place as the individual sees the need for them by virtue of his increasing learning about himself, and by the demands of each new environment situation. These kinds of changes are meaningful and can be expected to be permanent because they occur as an incidental reaction of the individual to his own increasing maturity and to the environmental forces around him. Behavior changes occur somewhat unconsciously and as a part of the total development process, and not in response to a specifically arranged procedure. The counselor places considerable confidence in the individual, but he also utilizes his persuasive capabilities to encourage client action. It is through involvement in a number of stimulating experiences that the individual makes many needed behavioral changes naturally and comfortably.

6. Individual freedom. The concept of individual freedom has, of course, a certain appeal for all theories, including those that don't provide for it very well. The problem is one of definition, combined with the facts that freedom is relative and that it varies considerably in degree. So, for a theory or counseling approach to espouse freedom doesn't mean much in and of itself.

Growth counseling utilizes the concept of freedom as a stated principle that serves as a guide in structuring the total counseling relationship. Freedom is seen as essentially an attitude, and the implications that one sees as outcomes of his particular perception of freedom are given special attention. Counseling is thus concerned with the development of a sense of freedom and with helping the individual sharpen those skills essential to his own continuing sense of freedom. Flexibility in thought, actions, and choices is accepted and encouraged, and the possible implications for any or all actions are carefully considered.

Summary

The trait-factor approach has a long history of notable contributions to counseling. Its focus upon the measurement of traits for the purpose of directing an individual toward a particular vocational goal has provided the needed guidelines for some effective counseling. The gathering and utilizing of pertinent data as a background to decision making have also proven useful.

The techniques used in counseling are relatively clear-cut, as they provide for the presentation and interpretation of accumulated data. The methods used are normally direct, but with encouragement of client participation in decision making.

Growth counseling utilizes many of the concepts and techniques of this approach, but views assessment as only a minor part of a counseling relationship. The stress is upon individual growth and upon the full utilization of all of one's capabilities for full individual development.

Williamson and the Minnesota point of view represent essentially the same philosophy and approaches as the trait-factor approach, but they also have some unique characteristics. Considerable stress is given to one's striving to become that of which he is capable. Counseling is a form of teaching that encompasses any and all approaches that may be potentially useful to the client. Self-actualization, behavior change, and freedom are all goals of this approach.

The five steps of analysis, synthesis, diagnosis, counseling, and follow-up characterize the rather formalized counseling approaches used. Advising, suggesting, and persuading are used and deemed advisable.

Growth counseling subscribes to much of the philosophy underlying this approach and utilizes to a moderate degree some of the techniques. It places considerably more stress upon the encouragement of achievements beyond the range of normal expectations. It taps and develops all potentialities and stresses a self-confidence that places no limits upon an individual's possible accomplishments.

Study and discussion problems

1. Identify some of the people who have been responsible for the development of the trait-factor theory. Relate something of interest about each of these people.
2. Compare this theory with any of the other theories with which you are now acquainted.
   a. Point out the similarities.
   b. Point out the differences.
3. How relevant do you feel the concept of traits is to decision making in the life of an individual? Explain.
4. Enumerate the traits of an individual about which you would be most concerned as an employer. How well do these traits lend themselves to measurement?
5. Review the techniques discussed in the chapter that are commonly used with this approach, and then add some additional ones.

6. Identify what you regard as the major strengths and most critical limitations of this approach.

References

Patterson, C. H. 1966, 2nd ed., 1973. *Theories of counseling and psychotherapy.* New York: Harper and Row. Pp. 6–48.

Shertzer, B., and Stone, S. C. 1968, 2nd ed., 1974. *Fundamentals of counseling.* Boston: Houghton Mifflin Company. Pp. 244–259 (1968); Pp. 181–184 (1974).

/ 8 /

Developmental counseling

Developmental counseling is broad in its conceptualization of what counseling is, and it is thorough in its utilization of the developmental process as a focus of counseling. This being the case, it may be regarded as a philosophical concept or a notion underlying much of education, rather than as a separate theory or counseling approach.

Human development, as the focus of this approach, is seen as a pattern of human experiences, as it involves those change processes in the physical, mental, and emotional components of personality that are continuous and that proceed in an orderly direction (Blocher 1966; 1968). Since changes are constantly taking place in the individual and in his environment, adjustment to these changes constitutes one of the great challenges of life.

Background

Although many of the ideas of developmental counseling have been known and accepted for a long time, this approach has only recently been recognized by some as a separate theory worthy of consideration.

Not all theories books give it coverage, however, in the same fashion as the more conventional approaches. Its chief proponents, Don Blocher and Don Dinkmeyer, have given considerable effort to defining and refining this approach.

The focus of developmental counseling during its short history has been upon the goals of self-understanding, awareness of one's potentialities, and methods of utilizing one's capacity (Dinkmeyer and Caldwell 1970). It is a form of personalized learning, but not individualized teaching, and its focus is upon prevention rather than remedy.

Major theoretical elements

The facilitation of the developmental process is the underlying force and motivation of this approach. It is felt by its exponents that if an individual is given assistance in developing and utilizing his potentialities many problems may be avoided. It is the counselor's function to provide children with information and direction by which they may better deal with developmental problems. This being the case, this approach is particularly useful with children.

Main themes of this approach

Like other approaches, developmental counseling has elements similar to those in other approaches, but it also has elements that tend to distinguish it from other approaches. Every person with an interest in developing a new theory or approach strives to identify some unique elements in his work.

The following include some commonalities with other theories, while still presenting some relatively unique ideas.

1. Dual focus on process and product. A dual focus is given to process and product in any attempted intervention with behavior (Blocher 1968). Behavior patterns are regarded as life stages through which the child moves rather than as final products. Each new pattern of behavior, then, provides some direction for the succeeding stages of development. That which occurs developmentally provides a framework or a base for a continuation of development.

2. Nature of human motivation. Man is not limited to reacting as a tension-reducing animal, but in reality reacts to a stimulus hunger as a driving force for action. He is motivated to control the environment and thus manage the sources of its stimulation, and does not limit himself to a mere reduction of stimulation in the environment. He thus reacts to a need for stimulation for its sake, and he also manipulates the environment to his best advantage.

3. Goals of counseling. Increasing self-understanding, a keener awareness of potentialities, and the organization of methods for utilizing one's capacities are the goals of counseling (Dinkmeyer 1966). Personal responsibility for one's decisions is stressed as the outcome of what the individual learns about himself and about his possibilities.

4. A collaborative relationship. The counseling relationship is basically collaborative between the counselor and client, both giving careful consideration to the problem and then deciding together how best to proceed. The individual has considerable freedom in decision making, with the counselor's function being one of assisting the individual as best he can with his developmental problems. Although the approach is essentially nonevaluative, it does provide the necessary structure to achieve a logical decision.

5. Development of a lifestyle. The child is seen as constantly in the process of developing a lifestyle, which in reality constitutes a way of life for him. Emphasis is given to the establishment of a positive self-concept, which is an essential force in avoiding anxiety and its negative influence upon performance.

6. The maximization of effectiveness. The maximizing of human effectiveness through a facilitation of the developmental process (Blocher 1966) is the ultimate goal of counseling. Counseling thus capitalizes upon the developmental process as a central means for assisting the individual. The personality unfolds in a healthy interaction between the organism and the environment, thus resulting in an appropriate developmental pattern. Development is thus seen as a source of stimulation and direction from which behavior changes are made, and the individual makes the most of his opportunities.

7. Freedom and the human experience. Freedom to choose, to grow, and to act is viewed as a vital part of the human experience. The counseling provided is directed toward helping the individual maximize his possible freedoms within the limitations of himself and his environment. A goal of counseling is to avoid or resolve any possible threats to the individual that may interfere with his freedoms or deter him from full development.

Since the degree of threat to the individual's affective qualities is the key force in determining his adjustment capabilities (Thompson 1967), it is necessary that the counselor project himself into the child's perceptual interpretation of the situation. The less threat felt by the individual, the greater the chances for a good adjustment through appropriate coping behaviors.

Techniques of developmental counseling

The techniques to be used under any theory are often implied, or they become evident to the counselor as his understanding of the theory increases. However, there is still merit in attempting to specifically identify the more common techniques. This approach stresses client responsibility, but in conjunction with considerable counselor involvement. Considerable attention is given to behavior change as the need becomes evident. Such change is in keeping with the developmental process and with the individual's potentialities.

Basic techniques include exploration, examination, and resolution (Dinkmeyer 1966) as means for resolving any existing developmental problems. Study and survey are used in gaining information to be used in making decisions, and also in identifying the available courses of action. Problem-solving techniques are also taught to the client, and suggestions are made about how he might best proceed. Reflection of feelings is used as a device for clarifying and coming to a better understanding of one's emotions and attitudes.

Developmental counseling and guidance (Dinkmeyer and Caldwell

1970) is broad and inclusive in its philosophy and techniques. This theory continues to elicit many implications for the counselor and for the classroom teacher. Much of its philosophy and many of its elements have a close relationship to the concept of growth counseling as described in this book.

A critique of developmental counseling

There is considerable merit to be found in developmental counseling, as it draws from many of the creditable elements of other theories and as it stresses a utilization of the developmental process. The pioneering efforts of its proponents have been most influential in adding to and changing counseling thought and practice.

Responses to this theory

Growth counseling rejects very little of the philosophy or concepts of this theory. The differences are found in the additional stress growth counseling places upon certain elements, and even more significantly, in the fact that growth counseling goes well beyond the concepts of developmental counseling. It is not content to deal with just the problems associated with development, or to accept the limitations of working with the individual's development pattern.

1. Dual focus on process and product. The dual focus on process and product is good, as it combines two elements of the helping relationship for broader and more effective counseling. Although behavior patterns may indeed be life stages, we see behavior as an outcome of unmet needs that may have only a remote relationship to development of the individual. Such behavior may have little to do with the eventual development of a life stage. Behavior is flexible and continually changing as new needs and demands are encountered. The counselor is aware of the intricacies of development, but he does not necessarily attribute or associate a behavior to or with this process. He views behavior as a manifestation of personal expression, and he works closely with the child in assessing that behavior in terms of its value in meeting needs and achieving goals. Inappropriate behavior is not overlooked because it may have its origin in a life stage. There is nothing final or inevitable about a life stage or the behavior that is supposed to characterize it. The individual is encouraged, and indeed is expected, to utilize his own decision-making capabilities to assess the correctness of his behavior. This is done with any needed direction from the counselor.

2. *Nature of human motivation.* Human motivation is viewed as a driving force within the individual that requires expression and leads to fulfillment. Man does indeed react to a stimulus hunger, and in so reacting may engage in behaviors not necessarily acceptable to his society. Growth counseling is very much aware of this condition and attempts to provide suggestions leading to behaviors that will satisfy this need for stimulation. It also suggests alternative actions that hold promise for a fulfillment of this stimulus hunger. Environmental stimulation is of course of tremendous significance here, since there is a dependence upon the environment for stimulation. We, however, stress the productivity possibilities of the individual as found within his own internal resources, which prompt action toward need fulfillment. Counseling thus capitalizes upon the fact that the greatest thrills and rewards experienced by the individual come from a realization that he has given a task his best efforts and that his achievements are outcomes of his own commitments and ambitions. The stimulus-hunger concept, which is a need everyone feels for stimulating experiences, is thus met through the involvement of the individual in a number of exciting experiences.

3. *Goals of counseling.* The goals of counseling are in many respects quite similar within the various theories. For example, increasing self-understanding, a sense of personal responsibility, and wise behavioral changes are basic goals of most counseling. Of course, there are additional goals, and there are differences among theories as to the amount of emphasis given to these goals.

Growth counseling accepts these notions, but it goes well beyond the promotion of an awareness concerning one's potentialities, which is seen as merely a first step. Counseling is directed toward helping him develop these potentialities to the highest degree possible. He is also helped to see the vast possibilities open to him through a utilization of his present skills and capacities. The promotion of a positive attitude about oneself and an optimism for the future is also stressed in conjunction with a commitment to self-improvement and worthy accomplishments.

Counseling is also directed toward goal setting, based upon findings from preliminary study in which potentialities are identified. Whether or not one's potentialities or capacities may be increased is open to question, but there is no doubt that every individual can be helped toward a fuller development and utilization of his capacities. Exact assessment, then, is not necessary, but meaningful action is most essential.

4. A collaborative relationship. The notion of a collaborative relationship should mark any meaningful counseling or psychotherapy. The questions include the degree of counselor involvement and the quality of assistance he can provide. In growth counseling, the client is given considerable freedom in his mode of attack upon problems, but he is also given the benefit of the counselor's thinking in assessing the true nature of his problems and in deciding upon a course of action. The assistance given stresses an objective appraisal of the total situation and the wise and economical use of time. Any floundering on the part of the client is eliminated through positive counselor action and needed structuring. There is no encroachment of freedom, but in reality his freedom is enhanced as he is encouraged to utilize his capabilities for problem resolution and for greater achievements. The quality of the collaborative effort is found in the degree of stimulation and direction afforded the client by the counselor, and in what the client does as a result of this relationship.

5. Development of a lifestyle. A lifestyle is an inevitable outcome of every individual's efforts to live as effectively and meaningfully as possible. Growth counseling assumes that each individual is constantly in the process of developing qualities of commonality and uniqueness, and it capitalizes upon this assumption as a fundamental of effective counseling. However, the lifestyle is viewed as a very dynamic ever-changing phenomenon over which the individual has considerable control, and not as a rather final outcome of one's needs.

Counseling further assumes a wide involvement in many growth-promoting experiences from which will come some rather significant changes in one's views and attitudes. Thinking thus becomes more profound, logical, and productive, and behavior patterns are modified to more appropriately accommodate the expanding intellect and increasing maturity of the individual.

6. The maximization of effectiveness. Human effectiveness is no doubt improved through a facilitation of the developmental process. A logical capitalization upon the developmental process should be included in any theoretical approach. Making the most of one's physiological and psychological attributes should undoubtedly lead to an increase in one's effectiveness. Growth counseling goes well beyond this concept, however, as it emphasizes the idea that much more can be done for the facilitation of development than is normally done. The growing bud will indeed unfold, but in the case of human development, there is far more to be considered than this natural, inevitable unfolding process.

Growth counseling not only works to facilitate development but also methodically and imaginatively takes appropriate steps to take advantage of this process for the personal and direct benefit of the individual. Growth counseling identifies the elements and the details of development and then devises methods for both increasing and utilizing them.

7. Freedom and the human experience. Certain freedoms are inevitably essential to the welfare of the individual, as they hold the promise of continuing growth and progress. However, there are some radically different interpretations of the term. Growth counseling interprets freedom to mean an unlimited opportunity to learn about oneself and fellow human beings, and about the environment, and then to have a wider range of opportunities to apply and to utilize these learnings. Freedom also includes a sense of responsibility for one's thoughts and actions, and the responsibility to make the most of one's opportunities for growth and progress.

Under this philosophy and approach, any possible threats to freedom are reduced or countered by the individual's increasing strengths and his abilities to fully utilize the environment. Any reduction of or threat to freedom occurs as the individual himself fails to utilize his capacities for effective and productive behavior. A retardation of development is thus immediately overcome and development enhanced through positive efforts, appropriate self-discipline, and a full utilization of current abilities and capacities.

Summary

Developmental counseling incorporates a number of elements from current theories and approaches into a conceptual framework, which focuses upon a utilization of the developmental process as a system for helping others. The work of Don Blocher and Don Dinkmeyer has been particularly significant in the development of this approach.

The concepts of this approach stress a utilization of the developmental process in dealing with problems that frequently have their origin in this same process. By helping the person deal with his problems it is believed that his total development will be enhanced.

The techniques used are rather broad and inclusive, but they do stress an exploration of the current condition and then the plotting of a course of action designed to overcome the difficulties.

Growth counseling accepts many of the theoretical notions and explanations of developmental counseling. So, it isn't so much a matter of the differences in the two approaches as it is a case of growth counseling going beyond the rather inevitable limits imposed by developmental counseling. Growth counseling includes a wide spectrum of possibilities as underlying contributors to human problems, regarding the developmental process as only one of these. The nature of the environment is a critical factor here. Growth counseling also stresses a full utilization of the developmental process as a source of assistance to an individual with problems. It focuses upon helping the individual develop and then capitalize upon his own internal resources for problem resolution and for continuous growth.

Study and discussion problems

1. Provide any information you can about the people most closely associated with this theory.
2. Review each of the seven characteristics of developmental counseling, and point out some implications that each has for the counselor.
3. Identify some elements in this approach that have important implications for counseling. Explain or describe some of these important implications for counseling.
4. Review the critique of this theory and then identify areas of agreement and disagreement that you have with the critique.
5. Identify what appear to be the most promising elements of this theory.

References

Blocher, D. H. 1966. *Developmental counseling.* New York: Ronald Press.

Dinkmeyer, D. C., and Caldwell, C. E. 1970. *Developmental counseling and guidance.* New York: McGraw-Hill.

Rational-emotive therapy

Rational-emotive therapy (RET) is something of a newcomer to counseling and psychotherapy, having its start about 1955 with a series of papers written by Dr. Albert Ellis. It is regarded by many therapists as something of a protest against the more traditional psychotherapeutic methods, and as an attempt to simplify the healing process.

Basic to this theory is the belief that irrational, neurotic learning acquired early in life persists, and that the absence of reinforcement does not necessarily result in the extinction of an unwanted attitude or behavior. Although the behavior itself is not reinforced, the individual persists in the reinforcement of these early learnings through a reindoctrination process that includes his telling himself how unworthy and no good he is. So, he continues to behave irrationally because of his illogical thoughts about himself.

Background

Albert Ellis (1913–   ) is the father and power behind rational-emotive therapy. His long and eventful history as a psychotherapist, author, and teacher, following the earning of his Ph.D. at Columbia in 1947, has provided him with experiences upon which he confidently builds his system. His disenchantment with the Freudian techniques, following his own personal analysis, led to a system that he felt would speed up the therapeutic process and give his patients something tangible with which to work. This movement toward a new system was characterized by a direct and even authoritarian involvement with the patient. He saw little sense in continuing to see a patient over a long period of time waiting for him to gain some insights, when Ellis was sure he knew what was wrong and what he should tell the patient in order to correct the difficulty.

His marriage and family counseling therapy with a variety of patients suffering from great numbers of emotional difficulties, and his writing, all contributed to the development of an innovative system of psychotherapy. Its influence is currently felt throughout the world of counseling and psychotherapy, even by those who may not subscribe to its tenets.

Major theoretical elements

Like all theories, rational-emotive therapy has certain underlying philosophical views. An understanding of these views contributes to one's comprehension of the concepts within the theory and increases the application possibilities of the concepts to therapy. Its central theme is that man is uniquely rational and also uniquely irrational (Ellis 1962). Emotional disturbances are the result of man's thinking illogically or irrationally. To overcome these disturbances and to improve his effectiveness, he must maximize his rational and minimize his irrational thinking. The contention persists within this theory that man can improve his situation considerably through logical thought and self-discipline. He needn't continue in a state of emotional upset, but in reality he can improve his situation by telling himself logical rather than illogical things about himself.

Major concepts of this theory

The principal concepts of this theory follow a rather precise pattern. These are based upon the A, B, C system, which in effect reveals the following about this theory: "A" represents the individual's act or behavior; "B" is what the person tells himself as a result of the behavior; and "C" is the consequence of that behavior. For example, a young man may ask a young lady for a date (A); he concludes that he must be no darn good (B), because she turns him down (C); otherwise why would she turn him down?

So, it isn't what really happens as a result of a behavior, but rather what the person tells himself about the behavior that causes the difficulty. So long as the person persists in attributing negative attributes to himself, thus blaming himself, he will continue to experience emotional difficulties.

1. Irrationality underlies emotionality. An emotional disturbance is caused by irrational thought. It is what the person thinks about a situation and his perceptions of himself in relationship to a situation that cause emotional difficulties. If the person could be completely rational and logical in his perceptions and in what he tells himself, no disturbance would need to occur. However, man is frequently illogical and self-deprecating in his thoughts, thus causing the emotional difficulty.

2. The relationship between emotions and thoughts. Human emotions and thoughts are so closely related as to be never completely separated, and are thus regarded as essentially the same thing. The fundamental life operations of sensing, moving, emoting, and thinking are experienced together, never in isolation. Ellis draws from Arnold (1960), who concludes that emotion is a complex process that starts when something is perceived and appraised. The appraisal creates a tendency to draw toward or away from the object or event according to its attractiveness.

3. The origin of irrational thinking. Irrational thinking has its origin with early learning influenced somewhat by a biological disposition toward bad logic, but more particularly by the influence of the culture. The child, then, learns certain attitudes about himself and his environment in response to others around him. He is frequently made to feel inferior and incompetent as he is subjected to criticism and abuse. The conclusions he reaches about himself are in reality logical in terms of the negative influences of others, but illogical in terms of his true worth and ability.

4. The use of symbols in thinking. Thinking is done through the use of symbols, which, in fact, is language. It is through this language that the individual tells himself illogical things about himself.

Sustained negative emotions are the result of stupidity, ignorance, or disturbance, and they can be overcome through the intelligent use of knowledge and correct thinking (Ellis 1962). The verbalization of positive thoughts then becomes necessary.

5. Self-verbalization and disturbance. Self-verbalizations, or what the individual continues to tell himself, contribute to emotional disturbance. Associated with this is the matter of how the individual perceives a situation and himself in relationship to the situation. Frequently the perception is inaccurate and self-effacing, and the individual's emotions are highly negative. The therapist assumes, then, that the patient is potentially capable but that he is defeating his own purposes through irrational reasoning. Negative emotions and disturbances may thus be overcome by getting the individual to verbalize positive statements about himself, and to desist from ever making a negative statement about himself.

6. A reorganization of perceptions. Self-defeating thoughts and emotions may be overcome through a reorganization of perceptions and more positive, rational thinking. Since false perceptions contribute to the difficulty, correct perceptions should result in more logical thinking. It is from this condition that the individual is able to progress toward a state of better adjustment.

The techniques of rational-emotive therapy

The actual techniques of this approach are in reality outcomes of the underlying philosophies. In other words, the therapist uses whatever techniques hold the greatest promise for changing the thinking of the individual. The idea is to get him to the point at which he will think more logically, realistically, and optimistically about himself, and at which he will tell himself only positive things about himself. Any technique that will accomplish this goal is acceptable.

For example, Ellis (1962) identifies eleven illogical ideas that he says contribute to a self-defeating attitude or to neurosis. These all stress the notion that the expectations of most people for themselves and for others are unrealistic and illogical. The purpose of therapy is to overcome these illogical thoughts and to think more logically about oneself and about the environment.

✗ The concepts of this theory suggest that the therapist uses a rather direct approach involving the giving of direction, the free use of advice marked by a very intellectual and persuasive attack upon the problem. The techniques are clear-cut and precise, and are characterized by objectivity and logic. The therapist persists in unmasking the patient's illogical thoughts and self-defeating verbalizations. This is done by forcefully bringing them to his attention, explaining to him how they are causing his disturbance, demonstrating the illogical links in his internalized sentences, and teaching him how to rethink, challenge, contradict, and reverbalize his sentences so that his thoughts become more logical and efficient (Ellis 1962). Instruction is an essential technique here, as the patient is taught how to think straight and to act effectively.

These same techniques are used with children. When the counselor is aggressively challenging, he is able to make a child see the faulty logic of his thinking (Glicken 1968). The aim is to improve functioning through this rather direct confrontation technique.

A critique of rational-emotive therapy

It is not difficult to find both merits and limitations in this theory. The notion that many of an individual's difficulties, as well as his emotional instability and inefficiency, have their roots in illogical thinking and in what the individual tells himself makes good sense. There is no reason to question this concept. However, this appears to be an overgeneralization and to have no more than a remote relationship to the causes of some individuals' problems. Growth counseling functions under the assumption that each person is unique and that causes of problems and difficulties may also be unique to the individual. It sees no simple explanation for the causes of behavior, particularly for the causes of neurosis and psychosis. The focus upon a central condition as a cause of maladaptive behavior fits the pattern of rational-emotive therapy but is viewed by growth counseling as an oversimplification of a very complex problem. There may be merit in focusing upon a relatively simple explanation for behavior, but this may be misleading to the individual seeking treatment, and thus not very helpful.

A response to rational-emotive therapy

The six main elements of this theory are considered separately as we respond in terms of the concepts of growth counseling.

1. Irrationality underlies emotionality. Irrationality may indeed contribute to emotionality, if the individual is permitted to reach a state of irrationality, and if he is not given immediate assistance aimed at overcoming these thoughts. Growth counseling believes the key to the problem of irrationality is found in a technique that constantly bolsters the self-esteem of the individual. If he tells himself irrational nonsense about himself, it is because he has lost confidence in himself and in his ability to handle threatening situations. Therefore, growth counseling stresses the proper use of one's intellectual resources and of one's strengths as a human being.

As emphasis is given to positive thinking about oneself and one's environment, the chances for the occurrence of illogical thinking of sufficient magnitude to constitute a threat are rather remote. The individual's continuing self-confidence serves to discourage the intrusion of illogical thoughts or feelings. Logic, balance, and stability in thought and action prevail as the person learns to believe in himself and in his environment, and as he learns to deal with threats to his well-being. Any tendency toward illogical thinking is handled by capitalizing upon the positive elements of the individual's personality, and by helping him achieve some needed successes as a bulwark to discouragement.

2. The relationship between emotions and thoughts. There is indeed a close relationship between emotions and thoughts. No attempt is made in growth counseling to achieve a separation of the two, but still there is a realization that there are some differences. Thought number one is not the same as emotion number one, but each has a direct influence upon the other. Growth counseling accepts each client as unique in his emotional and intellectual make-up and treats each one as a total unit comprised of a number of individual but interrelated personality traits.

Any attention given to one element of an individual's make-up is justified by the promise such action holds for helping the individual as a whole. He functions as a unit with many reciprocating elements, the isolation of which is deemed unnecessary. Total increasing maturity within a concept of wholeness remains the goal. Any unwanted behavior, which may be a reflection of illogical thinking, is eliminated indirectly through a close, ego-building relationship with the individual. His behavior then changes, not because the therapist has so instructed him to change, but because he is able to see the need for change in terms of his increasing self-confidence and because of the maturing process he is experiencing.

3. The origin of irrational thinking. The origin of much of the irrational thinking of which many of us are guilty may, indeed, rest with the learning of early childhood. It may be too late for preventive measures, but it is not too late for effective treatment. Since he learned to think irrationally as a victim of his environment, and of himself, so, too, may he learn to think rationally. Certainly, the environment of the typical child is not entirely conducive to full development and effective functioning. We know that there are many circumstances within the life of every child that tend to reduce rather than bolster self-esteem and that threaten the child's security. Some illogical thinking and rationalizations may occur as the child is thwarted in meeting his needs and in gaining essential satisfactions.

Growth counseling focuses upon a reduction of the negative influences of any existing undesirable environmental conditions upon the individual by directing him to look to himself for the needed strengths and abilities. Thus, instead of capitulating to environmental conditions, which may not be subject to control, the individual improves and magnifies his own adjustment and productive resources. Logical thought and actions are the outcomes of this state of independence, courage, and self-confidence.

4, 5. The use of symbols in thinking; self-verbalization and disturbance. Since thinking is done through the use of symbols, counseling should give attention to the thought processes and to the language through which thoughts are expressed. Growth counseling encourages and provides for the facilitation of language usage as a means for expressing one's thoughts and actions. Each individual is aided in developing his language skills and in finding appropriate terms with which to express himself. He is then directed in using positive terms and expressions to describe himself and to magnify the concept of his worthiness. Language is thus utilized as a method for developing self-esteem and bolstering self-confidence. The possibilities that the individual will verbalize illogical thoughts about himself while he enjoys a high level of self-confidence are rather remote.

Any emotional disturbances to occur as a result of negative comments about oneself are avoided as the individual learns to make only positive comments and as faith in himself continues to grow. The continuous use of self-deprecating terms is indefensible for even the relatively insecure individual. The new insights gained, skills developed, and achievements realized all tend to bolster the self-confidence, thus resulting in continually more effective functioning.

6. A reorganization of perceptions. A reorganization of perceptions is, indeed, essential to improved mental health. The problem is one of ascertaining and applying the techniques most likely to achieve this goal. Rational-emotive therapy depends to a high degree upon intellectual explanations and upon verbal assignments provided by the therapist. Growth counseling depends more upon providing experiences, encouragement, and reinforcement as devices for building the self-esteem which will inevitably lead to more positive self-perceptions.

Self-defeating attitudes and verbalizations are largely avoided in growth counseling, but are dealt with both directly and indirectly if they do occur. They are dealt with directly by encouraging the person to talk freely about his feelings and by involving him in activities with ego-developing possibilities. Indirect benefits accrue from the person's increasing self-confidence. He may not know why he is less negative about himself or why is he able to say more good things about himself, but it does happen by virtue of his total increasing abilities and his greater self-confidence.

The promise of a better theory

Rational-emotive therapy has provided a framework for a stronger and more promising theory. It has identified certain elements of the personality and conditions of neurosis, which, as they become better understood, can be dealt with more adequately. It has stimulated thought and experimentation, which has and will continue to have an impact upon psychological thought. The counselors and psychotherapists who subscribe to this theory will undoubtedly become more proficient and increasingly more effective by virtue of their experiences. Those who do not follow this approach may nevertheless profit from the ideas it presents.

Growth counseling draws from this theory for ideas and possibilities for the development and refinement of new theory. It also provides for an extension of the ideas under RET in an effort to develop a system more compatible with the needs and peculiarities of individual clients, and more in keeping with existing conditions within the society.

Summary

Rational-emotive therapy has enjoyed a rather popular acceptance, due in part to the dynamic and enthusiastic leadership provided by Dr. Albert Ellis, and in part to the appeal of the ideas presented.

This theory sees neurosis and psychosis as outcomes of irrational thoughts. It is what the person tells himself that constitutes the heart of the difficulty, and not the event itself. As the person continues to tell himself that he is stupid, no good, and unworthy, he is unable to overcome his emotional problems and difficulties.

The techniques of this approach are characterized by a direct confrontation approach that includes explanations and rather forceful direction on how to overcome a problem. Emphasis is given to intellectualization, logic, and reason in determining the causes of a problem and in deciding how to proceed in order to overcome it.

Growth counseling accepts the idea that a neurosis may be intensified through negative verbalizations. It relies, however, upon providing growth-promoting experiences and upon positive encouragement and reinforcement to avoid a low self-esteem, which then prompts negative thoughts about oneself. It utilizes the same principles in helping the individual overcome any existing negativism about self.

Language development is stressed as a means for encouraging the individual to express his feelings and as a system for bolstering self-confidence and self-esteem.

Study and discussion problems

1. Describe Albert Ellis as a person and as a professional. Relate what you know about him as a person with some of the elements of his theory.
2. Identify some of the philosophical elements that characterize this theory. To what extent do you feel a theory depends upon philosophy?
3. Develop your own critique of each of the six main concepts of this theory.
4. Demonstrate the use of this theory in an actual counseling or role-playing situation.

References

Corsini, R., ed. 1973. *Current psychotherapies.* Itasca, Illinois: F. E. Peacock. Pp. 167–206.

Ellis, A. 1962. *Reason and emotion in psychotherapy.* New York: Lyle Stuart.

Patterson, C. H. 1966, 2nd ed., 1973. *Theories of counseling and psychotherapy.* New York: Harper and Row Pp. 49–76.

Shertzer, B., and Stone, S. C. 1974. *Fundamentals of Counseling.* Boston: Houghton Mifflin Company. Pp. 184–188.

/ 10 /

Reality therapy

Reality therapy does not appear in most of the theory books; however, no matter what its current status with theorists may be, it does have much to offer the counselor and psychotherapists today.

The sound concepts of this theory have value in making other theories more understandable and useful.

The core of the philosophy underlying this theory is that each individual must be responsible for his own actions. This says, in effect, that if the individual is in trouble, it is because of his failure to live by the rules and to assume responsibility for himself and for his actions.

Background

Reality therapy had its initiation with Dr. William Glasser, a California psychiatrist, whose experiences in private practice and as a consultant to a number of schools prompted the belief that traditional psychotherapeutic procedures were not adequate for today's world. This theory is, at least in part, a protest against conventional theories (Glasser 1965) and an attempt to develop a more logical approach for helping people stay out of trouble and live more effective lives. More recent publications (Glasser 1969; 1972) expand upon this philosophy and reflect an increasing confidence by Glasser and the public in this theory.

Its relatively brief history has been characterized by varying degrees of success in the Ventura School for Girls in California, in private practice, and even in its application to the classroom.

Major theoretical elements

The importance of a person's realizing a degree of success in this life is emphasized throughout the concepts of this theory. It is believed that if the person is able to feel good about himself, and about his relationships with other people, he will be able to handle most of his problems satisfactorily.

Main concepts of this theory

The principal elements of this theory embrace the philosophy and ideas already expressed, as well as presenting a number of tenets in a pattern designed to give meaning and purpose to life. This pattern includes the need that everyone has to feel that he is a worthy human being capable of resolving his problems and living effectively. It also stresses the notion that a person must be responsible for himself and that there is no such thing as neurosis, as commonly defined. If a person is in trouble, it is because he has behaved inappropriately, not because he is ill. Such rationalizations are not acceptable in this theory.

1. Feelings of success. It is most essential that the individual feel successful and that he experience real success in some aspect of his life (Glasser 1969). His general success and various achievements depend upon a deep realization that he is capable of doing something well. With such feelings, the person will continue to function well, and there will be no need for "patching up" procedures, which are notably unsuccessful anyway. The goal of therapy is to get the individual responsibly and meaningfully involved in activities that hold considerable promise for success. It is from this background that the person learns to feel capable and is able to meet the demands of his society.

2. Giving and receiving love. The basic needs of the individual include being loved and having the opportunity to love others. Hopefully, the educational enterprise and society itself will gear themselves to meet this vital need of all its citizens.

Loneliness does not just happen, it is the natural outcome of failure. The avoidance of loneliness and its accompanying problems is found in a close relationship with other humans. Such relationships contribute to self-confidence and to the minimization of frustration, which so frequently leads to unhappiness and withdrawal. A failure to identify with others and to have warm, close, personal relationships contributes to loneliness and to a relatively barren and unproductive existence.

3. Reason, logic, and behavior. Although emotions have a place in life, reason and logic are the ingredients essential to appropriate behavior and for the individual's success. To be misled by emotion is to invite failure. In reality, emotion is the result of behavior, thus the need to improve behavior in order to avoid inappropriate emotions (Glasser 1969). It is the purpose of therapy to help the individual find a better way to behave. He is then expected to make such a commitment and to follow through on it.

4. Inability to meet needs. The adjustment difficulties of many individuals rest with their inability to meet needs. The symptoms of this inadequacy are manifested in a variety of fashions by different people. However, these symptoms generally disappear once the individual is successful in fulfilling his needs. The individual who finds himself thwarted in his attempts to fulfill needs has a tendency to deny the reality of the world. He blames others, and he fails to realize that his problems could be resolved through more responsible behavior.

5. Overcoming feelings of inadequacy. So much of a person's so-called misbehavior is due to his feeling inadequate and incapable of dealing with his problems. If the two basic needs of the individual, to love and be loved and to feel worthwhile to oneself and to others, are not met, feelings of inadequacy are the result. The solution to these feelings of inadequacy is found in the person's learning how to meet needs. Hopefully, this is achieved through therapy. The ideal situation is for the individual to have the opportunity from infancy on to know how to meet needs. If these feelings do develop, then they must be overcome if the person is to function effectively.

6. *Personal responsibility.* A sense of personal responsibility for oneself and for one's actions is essential to the successful life. To be responsible is the ability to fulfill personal needs while not depriving others of the opportunity to do likewise (Glasser 1965). Unlike the animal, which relies upon instinct for survival, man must depend upon his mentality. It is through his capacity to increase his mental capabilities that man is able to avoid and resolve problems. The conditions essential to an individual's learning to be responsible include exposure to love and discipline and to appropriate instructions from adults early in life.

Techniques of reality therapy

The techniques used in this theory are directed at helping the individual face reality and fulfill his needs. Therapy thus includes teaching and direct training in an effort to overcome any existing limitations of the person's past. It is felt that appropriate training in childhood and a desirable environment will prevent many problems. If conditions have not been favorable, then therapy is necessary.

Involvement marks the relationship between the therapist and client, as there is a candid exchange of ideas. The therapist rejects the behavior manifested by the client, but without jeopardizing his involvement with the client. Instruction is used to explain and to show the person how to meet his needs in a realistic fashion.

A critique of reality therapy

Certainly, most of the fundamental concepts of reality therapy make good sense and are acceptable to growth counseling. The matter of personal responsibility is critical to the welfare of any individual and indeed to society itself. Being capable of giving and receiving love, and of enjoying feelings of importance, are likewise important to the mental health of the individual.

A response to reality therapy

Despite the merits of this approach, both philosophically and psychologically, it still has some fundamental weaknesses and some apparent limitations that cannot be ignored. It is easy, for example, to say what should be the case in the life of an individual, but this does not solve the problem for him. Nor is it difficult to take the position that each individual should assume the major responsibility for himself. How to get him to act responsibly when he refuses to do so, despite explanations and threats and his own insights that he could do so, is equally baffling.

Under the growth-counseling concept, the possibilities for achieving the excellent goals of reality therapy are increased considerably. There is a greater reliance upon the development of self, and upon the internal resources of self, upon which the individual can depend for both avoiding and resolving problems. The key to good adjustment is found in the quality and strength the individual sees in himself.

1. Feelings of success. Feelings of success are indeed essential for full and productive functioning. These feelings are attainable through appropriate efforts and the sense of pride that comes from the realization of achievements, which occurs as the product of these efforts. The sense of pride that accompanies the knowledge that one has done his best is a genuine augmentor of positive feelings. The individual need not be first in every endeavor, nor need his achievements be of top quality. It is important that a task receive his best efforts, and that he can take honest pride in a job well done.

Growth counseling fosters this sense of pride in both counseling sessions and in other related activities designed to promote growth and increase skills. Direction is provided through explanations, reflection of feelings, assignments, and structuring with the assumption that worthy achievements will result. The thrill of accomplishment and the feelings of importance thus follow the dedicated efforts of the individual. The permanence of these feelings becomes evident as the individual continues to capitalize and build upon preceding successes. These feelings of importance are based upon wholehearted efforts and upon sacrifices that pay off in personal feelings of elation and personal pride.

2. Giving and receiving love. The ability to receive and to give love is, of course, fundamental to happiness and to success. As an ideal this is fine, but realistically this condition is rarely achieved to a desirable degree. This being the case, the individual must learn to adjust to a condition that includes an absence of love from others in his environment, and to a condition that does not always permit him an expression of love for others. He must therefore look to himself for the satisfactions that are not readily forthcoming from others. He can think of himself and believe in himself as a worthy human being, despite the absence of love from others. This condition is not regarded as a substitute for love, which is of course an important element in life, but as a way to compensate for gaps in one's existence.

In growth counseling, the client is also taught the skills and attitudes that invite the love and attention of others and that result in one's being more acceptable to others and to oneself. He thus increases his chances for having his needs met, and he also minimizes the frustrations that may occur when his needs are not met.

3. Reason, logic, and behavior. Reason and logic should characterize all thinking and should obviously play an important part in decision making. So, too, is emotion an important element in the thought and decision-making processes. In growth counseling, there is the assumption that a separation of logic and emotion is neither possible nor desirable. It is safe to assume that both are present in most counseling encounters. The best resources of the individual are thus brought into play in resolving problems and in making plans, as he is regarded as a whole entity comprised of many elements of emotion and intellect. The counselor treats him accordingly, as he accepts him as a deserving, behaving individual with many possibilities for effective action and worthy accomplishment.

4. Inability to meet needs. The inability to meet needs is obviously a major contributing factor in emotional difficulties and various kinds of maladjustment. However, there is a problem of what constitutes a genuine need, and who determines the difference between a need and a wish. For example, an individual may be experiencing some serious adjustment problems, which may be due to unrealistic expectations of his environment or of himself. He may feel a "need" to be important and to have status, but if this is not possible under existing circumstances, then he should modify his expectations accordingly. A person may have the "need" to be loved, but if this need is not met to the degree expected by the individual, then he should make an appropriate adjustment to the condition and not permit a capitulation to an undesirable emotional state.

Self-discipline and self-control are a part of the picture here, but more importantly, the individual is utilizing his own emotional and intellectual resources for purposes of making a needed adjustment. Such self-discipline is not difficult for the individual who has learned to rely upon himself for the needed direction and strength for effective action.

5. Overcoming feelings of inadequacy. Feelings of inadequacy are of course devastating to the personality and constitute serious deterrents to effective functioning. It is also understandable that misbehavior frequently occurs with individuals suffering from such feelings. This being the case, growth counseling has as a major goal the prevention of such feelings. This is done by providing the kinds of experiences that constantly bolster self-esteem and add to the self-confidence of the individual. The positive aspects of personality development receive the attention of the counselor, and the individual is constantly encouraged toward and reinforced for appropriate actions and high achievements.

The inevitability of some feelings of inadequacy is, of course, recognized by the counselor and such feelings are handled in much the same way as other feelings. The client is encouraged to express himself freely, but he is also expected to identify the possible causes for these feelings and to provide some suggestions on how to overcome them. The counselor does more than reflect feelings, as he sees reflection as only a first step toward the gaining of insights and the concerted action taken to overcome a difficulty.

6. *Personal responsibility.* Personal responsibility, as the heart of reality therapy, may well be emulated by all counseling approaches. The notion that the individual must learn to be responsible for himself and assume the consequences of his behavior makes good sense. The problem is one of oversimplification. If everyone were to observe this concept, the world would indeed be a different place in which to live. But it is a fact that a substantial number of individuals do not recognize the meaning or importance of this notion, nor do they learn how to apply it. Growth counseling recognizes this fact and attempts both to teach this concept and to deal with individuals who may never fully accept or practice the notion of personal responsibility.

As growth counseling concentrates upon the building of self-confidence, it is assumed that the development of a sense of responsibility will occur as a concomitant to increasing self-confidence. As the individual learns to believe in himself, he is better prepared for and more likely to assume the major responsibility for his total self within his society. The concept of total growth espoused here relies upon the individual's full utilization of his capacities, and upon the application of his capabilities to daily, effective living.

The future of reality therapy

The future of reality therapy is a very promising one. The concept of personal responsibility for one's own behavior has broad universal appeal. Many individuals feel that it is through a sense of individual responsibility that meaningful and permanent growth occurs.

Likewise, the idea that every youngster should succeed to his own sense of satisfaction makes sense. This belief has had a significant impact upon the attitudes of educators and upon educational practice.

The conceptual framework of reality therapy provides guidelines for improving the educational experiences of children. This structure thus transcends mere therapy and provides for a much broader coverage of aids by which behaviors may be changed and bettered.

Summary

Reality therapy had its beginning with Dr. William Glasser, who, in protest against conventional psychotherapy, attempted to explain human behavior. The notion is stressed that each individual must feel good about himself, feel that he is a worthy individual and capable of meeting his needs. Everyone must feel loved and be capable of giving love, and any failure in this regard leads to maladjustment.

A sense of personal responsibility, in which the individual is expected to recognize and abide by the reality of a situation, is the core of this theory. Logic and reason should guide one's behavior, and efforts must be directed toward meeting one's needs and overcoming any feelings of inadequacy.

Teaching, training, and telling are combined with other techniques in this theory. The individual is expected to follow instructions and to make an effort to overcome his difficulties. Explanations are made as to the reality of the situation, and the individual is put under some pressure to conform to community expectations.

The limitations of this theory are seen in its oversimplifications as to the causes and cures of maladjustment. A failure to conform leads to problems, and in order to avoid problems, one must conduct oneself properly. A person who finds himself in difficulty must then change his behavior.

Growth counseling concentrates upon the development of self-confidence, and upon the bolstering of self-esteem, with the belief that with total personal growth will come the insights and the abilities to avoid difficulties and to deal with them should they occur.

Study and discussion problems

1. How well does the word "reality" describe this theory? Explain how the term is being used.

2. Identify the concepts within this theory that appear to you to be quite different from any others you have known. Identify those concepts that are rather commonly known.
3. Add some additional concepts that you feel should be basic to any theory. How compatible is each of these with reality therapy?
4. Demonstrate this approach by role-playing a counselor with another person serving as the client. Be precise, and even dramatize your techniques, for purposes of showing your observers what these techniques are.

References

Corsini, R., ed. 1973. *Current psychotherapies.* Itasca, Illinois: F. E. Peacock. Pp. 287–315.

Glasser, W. 1965. *Reality therapy.* New York: Harper and Row.

Glasser, W. 1969. *Schools without failure.* New York: Harper and Row.

Glasser, W. 1972. *The identity society.* New York: Harper and Row.

Gestalt therapy

We are constantly faced with the challenge of determining which elements of a psychotherapeutic theory with a medical orientation have relevance for the counselor in an educational setting. The answer to this problem probably rests with attaching varying degrees of importance to the more acceptable elements. This is to say that there is neither an outright acceptance nor a complete rejection of these elements, but rather it is a matter of putting more emphasis upon some than upon others. Gestalt therapy provides this kind of a challenge.

There is a definite relationship between this therapy and some of the theories under the classification of learning theory. An even closer relationship is seen with classical psychoanalysis.

Background

The precise history of this therapy is perhaps not too clear since much of current gestalt therapy is an outcome or extension of other therapeutic approaches. Since its theoretical considerations may be found throughout man's written history, it is logical to assume that its offerings are not really original (Kempler 1973). The activities incorporated into this approach likewise have little to distinguish them from many other therapeutic approaches. Gestalt therapy, under the leadership of Dr. Frederick Perls, did establish an appropriate language and a framework of sorts from which to work. So this gives it some distinction worthy of note.

An earlier publication (Perls, Goodman, and Hefferline 1951) provided the background and structure for gestalt therapy. The gestalt theories about the organization of perception have been used in looking at a basis for mental disturbance, thus stressing the application of gestalt psychology to psychotherapy. Psychopathology is explained as a disturbance of figure-ground formation. In this case "figure" is the central element of attention in the individual's perceptual field, and "ground" is in the background of the field. What is "figure" may change rapidly, depending upon how an individual perceives a situation.

Gestalt psychology emerged essentially as a reaction against the fragmented and analytic orientations of the other psychologies. Its major thesis has been that the whole is not simply the sum of its parts, but something quite different from the parts alone. It is only through a consideration of the whole that the system of the individual can be understood. And it is only after the whole is understood that the parts can have meaning.

Major theoretical elements

Gestalt therapy sees inappropriate or disturbed behavior as a signal of a polarization between two elements in a psychological process (Kempler 1973). To resolve this condition it is necessary to bring the polarized or discordant elements into the open. It is through the process of open confrontation and self-disclosure that the individual's behavior is modified.

Awareness is stressed as the beginning of change. Awareness of self and of the present serves to prompt action toward growth and change.

The whole self is thus in creative contact with the environment. The goal of counseling is a reshaping of the individual's sensory capacities. This is done through an encouter with the therapist or with others in which there is an encouragement to be aware of feelings. Opportunity for self-discovery thus underlies this approach. As the individual in therapy is able to alter his perspective or sense of awareness, he is then able to change his behavior.

Main concepts of this theory

The concept of wholeness characterizes this approach, as considerable attention is given to the individual's functioning as a unified whole and to the notion that the various parts of any whole have meaning only as unified into a total pattern. The environment is also seen as a major influence in the life of the individual. It is within this organism-environment setting that the person learns to function.

1. Current reality. It is what exists now that is of major importance. It is the reality of the existing organism and of the environment today that attracts the attention of the therapist. Treatment, then, is directed toward the whole organism (Perls, Hefferline, and Goodman 1965) and toward the reality of the situation for the individual. Reality is seen as that aspect of one's life that dictates one's behavior. Perceptions are individual, thus calling for a consideration of personal needs in prescribing new courses of action for any one individual. It is through the organism-environment unity that the nature of the individual's relationship with his physical and social environment is determined and that decisions are made on how best to help him. If something within the environment is amiss or in disharmony with the organism, then efforts are made to bring the needed changes to the environment in order to more fully accommodate the organism.

2. The total organism and improvement. A person improves only as the total organism is affected and as the totality of the functioning is utilized. The therapist must direct his efforts toward the organized whole, or the gestalt of the individual, in effecting behavioral changes. Unity, integration, and wholeness are utilized in therapy, but they are also the goals of therapy. So the therapeutic relationship is characterized by breadth of thought, wholeness of the organism, and an integration of elements within the individual with the elements available in the environment.

Since the concept of "wholeness" is rather abstract, difficulty is experienced in explaining its relationship to the therapeutic process. It does suggest, however, the importance of experiencing and having an active part in the relationship with the therapist. Rather than just listening to the intellectual explanations and interpretations of the therapist with the hope of gaining some insights, the individual is provided opportunities for active involvement with the therapist. It is from this activity that the person experiences feelings from which meaningful behavior changes may occur.

3. The relationship with the environment. The interaction of the organism with the environment is basic to all behavior. In other words, behavior is determined to a degree by the nature of this relationship and by the individual's perception of himself and the environment. The individual's functioning is dependent upon objects and conditions within the environment. For example, anger is a result of obstacles to progress that evoke frustration. Functioning also depends upon reasoning directed at the resolution of problems. There is, then, an interacting within and between the organism and the environment. It is from this organism-environment unity that the individual gets his cues for behavior.

Gestalt therapy sees man as experiencing considerable discord within himself. The psychological processes are in disharmony, thus adding to his problems of adjustment. The environment is thus seen as holding possibilities for experiencing and for meaningful activities from which symptom amelioration may result. In other words, as the individual is permitted and encouraged to act and to interact with others within his environment, discordant elements are reduced and a more meaningful functioning results.

4. Acting as a whole. The unified, organized, integrated whole of the individual results in his behaving as a whole. Any consideration of the appropriateness of behavior should consider this notion. The condition of the individual that includes the human, the organism, and the environment has social as well as physical considerations. So, in the study of the individual, and in counseling, consideration must be given to the field in which the social, cultural, animal, and physical factors interact. Every problem, then, occurs in a social-animal-physical field.

Man is viewed as having a brain with the capacity to differentiate and conceptualize. This capacity, when properly utilized, contributes to wholeness in his actions. This capacity does depend, however, upon the phenomenon of "polarization" (Kempler 1973), which means a condition of opposites. For example, in order to describe *soft,* the individual must also know its opposite as found in the word *hard.* It is through an acceptance of a condition of polarization and its proper utilization that the individual's possibilities for functioning as a whole are enhanced.

5. The field of interaction. There is a field in which the sociocultural individual interacts with physical factors in the environment. The functioning of the individual within the environment provides a contact, which may be known as experience. All human functioning, then, is an interacting within an organism-environment field, which involves the sociocultural, the animal, and the physical. All contact is a kind of creative adjustment of the organism to itself and to the environment.

Experiencing thus receives considerable emphasis. It is through active involvement with others in meaningful kinds of emotion-evoking experiences that the individual is able to modify or abandon his symptoms of maladjustment or pathology. For example, the individual may be brought into actual physical contact with others in a therapy group in a feeling- or emotion-evoking encounter. Confrontation through verbal accusations or interpretations may also be made by the therapist or by a group member. Interaction with others thus constitutes the heart of the therapeutic process. This is sometimes accomplished by the use of games or confrontation exercises in which there is considerable involvement by the participants.

6. The nature of growth. Growth involves an awareness as to the existence of a field and is the result of the contact experienced by the organism with the environment within the total field. Growth is the function of the contact boundary within the organism-environment field. Through the creative function of adjustment, the organic units continue in the larger organization of the field. Growth is, therefore, broad, inclusive, and the result of dynamic forces within the individual and within the environment.

Man is seen as a part of a vital process in which he is happening. Rather than being an event, he is a process. Intelligent awareness and psychological awareness thus provide a structure for this process in which man is constantly in the process of becoming. The emphasis in treatment is thus open, providing for experiencing, from which the individual profits as he learns to recognize and accept feelings and as he translates these into constructive, growth-promoting behaviors.

The techniques of gestalt therapy

The techniques used are essentially the same as those used in some of the other approaches, except that this theory utilizes confrontation, questioning, telling, and instructing to a higher degree than is true in most of the other approaches. There are an abruptness and a lack of regard for the feelings of the client that characterize this approach. The therapist functions with considerable self-assurance and with an attitude that suggests that he knows what is best for the client, and there is no hesitation in his letting the client know this.

The therapist feels that it is his task to restore the personality of the client to his gestalt or to the organized whole (Perls, Hefferline, and Goodman 1965). This can be best accomplished through explanation, interpretations, instructions, and persuasion. Therapy involves analyzing the internal structure of the experience, and emphasis is given to the *how* of the experience, not the *what.* How the individual is reacting, behaving, remembering, and communicating is the important point here. The therapist strives to trigger client action, which he then evaluates, and from which a course of action is structured.

Whatever techniques are used, they are basic to the view that symptoms constitute a warning of difficulties within the process. Symptoms suggest some kind of distress within the living process of the individual. An amelioration of these symptoms becomes the goal.

Any tendency to block expression or feelings may be handled by encouraging a full expression of those feelings both verbally, and in some cases physically. The focus is thus upon interaction of the participants, including an energetic involvement by the therapist.

A critique of gestalt therapy

Growth counseling incorporates some of the philosophy of this approach in its total framework. This occurs, perhaps, more by accident than by design, since the concepts of growth counseling incorporate the notion of wholeness within a structural pattern that emphasizes the internal resources of the individual. In other words, the heart of growth counseling is the maximum development of the individual. The notion of "wholeness" is no doubt a part of this broad concept of growth.

A response to gestalt therapy

There are some rather precise differences between growth counseling and the point of view expressed in gestalt therapy, particularly in the techniques used. Other differences will be identified in the paragraphs to follow. Greater stress is given in growth counseling to the quality of the relationship, and little credence is given to abruptness or confrontation. Considerable credit is given to the assumed integrity and dignity of the client, and confidence in his ability to assist in the process is shown.

1. Current reality. What is current reality should of course be given careful consideration, despite the fact that no one may be able to determine this with any degree of assurance. So, one can see the client's first need in this respect as one of clarifying reality, since he may be very confused about it. His perceptions of what constitutes reality may differ markedly from the true situation as interpreted by society or by the therapist.

Therapy, under growth counseling, gives attention to the client's perceptions, but primarily for purposes of determining their accuracy, and assessing their worth as a therapeutic tool. Appropriate adjustments in thoughts and behavior then become the goals of therapy. Too frequently, in some approaches, the therapist willingly accepts reality as perceived by the client and then works from that position. It would seem that ultimate and lasting growth is more likely to be achieved if the client is aided in making a critical appraisal of his perceptions.

2. *The total organism and improvement.* A consideration of the total organism is of course essential in any approach. The concept of wholeness has merit, but a critical point here is one of permitting and even facilitating a careful look at all elements within the whole for purposes of identifying those with the greatest need for attention. The whole person remains so and performs at a level of efficiency only if all segments of the totality are in harmony and are augmenting each other; full functioning of the client is thus the immediate and the long-term goal of counseling, and the techniques utilized should be so directed.

3. *The relationship with the environment.* The relationship of the individual with the environment constitutes a dynamic influence for behavior. The organism-environment unity no doubt provides the cues for behavior. The individual, then, has a dual relationship. In one case it is with his true, dominant self, and the other is the relation the individual has with his environment. There is a need for harmony within the totality of the person, and a harmony between the person and his environment. The organism-environment unity can be accepted as a basis for the prompting of behavior, but only as one element. This unit can be seen as having merit only after it is combined with the controllable traits and behaviors of the individual. In other words, this concept cannot be accepted as inevitable or even fatalistic, but rather as an opportunity for the individual to make the most of himself through appropriate self-disciplining measures, and of the environment through necessary controls. Effective functioning is the goal here, and appropriate steps, within the framework of personal growth, should be taken to achieve this objective.

4. *Acting as a whole.* Acting as a unified whole is of course evident

with most individuals, and the need to treat each person accordingly is desirable. There is also the need to anticipate behavior that constitutes a reflection of this condition. A better understanding of the total personality, with an awareness of the various parts of that personality, is a constant goal of growth counseling. The counselor, then, explores with the client and probes for a clarification and a better understanding of the elements of the personality. Just to see and work with the person as a whole is not sufficient. A meaningful knowledge of the nature of the relationship between and among the various personality traits is essential to counselor and client, as background to more effective functioning.

5. The field of interaction. The field of interaction within which the person functions is obviously a major determinant of behavior. However, there are other dimensions to this concept. The individual need not be a victim of his perceptual field. He can help determine the nature of this field through his own imaginative creations, self-discipline, and environmental manipulation.

There is a recognition, then, that the individual is influenced by his society and his culture. However, the nature of that influence depends to a high degree upon what the person is and is in the process of becoming at any one time. In other words, he has some control over these influencing elements; he is not a helpless victim of himself or of the environment. As a sociocultural being, he reacts to the environment, but he also exercises certain controls over that same environment. There is more, then, to this condition than just contact between the individual and his environment. The environment is in a sense really a part of the individual, as he exercises considerable control over his fate. The "field" of the individual is very broad in this sense, as the person and his surroundings are essentially one, with no real need to separate the two.

The counselor, under these circumstances, accepts and provides the client the opportunity to clarify and come to a better understanding of all the influences in his life. Growth thus becomes a process of coming to a better understanding of self and of increasing one's ability to utilize the self and the environment more fully.

Contact between the individual and his surroundings does constitute experience, which can be meaningful if the individual is able to perceive elements in the environment as really parts of himself. There is a broadening of the concept of self here that will more adequately make each experience more meaningful and beneficial.

6. *The nature of growth.* Growth involves more than an awareness of the environment and the contacts experienced with that environment. The individual is expected to perceptively assess the total field of the environment and to make judgments about the relative merits of the elements within that environment. He is then expected to identify and utilize those elements holding the greatest promise for individual progress. This is not a by-chance condition, but rather one to be achieved through careful thought and trial.

The counselor facilitates this process as he provides some encouragement and direction in helping the person make a critical appraisal of himself and of his environment. He contributes to client growth as he provides the structure for activities that will make full use of the client's intellectual capacities. Decisions about behavior changes and about how best to utilize available resources are arrived at logically. Emotions are not ignored and are utilized as augmenting factors in decision making. Sound judgments, logical decisions, and appropriate action, in view of existing facts, are all immediate aims of the counselor.

The future of gestalt therapy

Gestalt therapy holds considerable promise for the future, particularly as greater emphasis is given in counseling and psychotherapy to the medical model. A rather direct attack upon one's problems has also been given greater emphasis by a number of approaches in recent years. Although gestalt therapy provides for considerable client freedom, it nevertheless stresses a candid look at prevailing problems and vigorous movement toward needed action.

Gestalt therapy is also profiting from the advancements being made in other approaches. The enrichment possibilities become evident as this therapy draws ideas from and is stimulated by other theoretical positions. As the need for a consolidation of ideas and the merging of techniques into a large comprehensive theory becomes more evident, gestalt therapy will continue to make its contributions felt.

The popularity of the behavioristic approaches has benefited the gestalt approach because of the similarities concerning learning as a means for changing behavior. The notion of wholeness also has some appeal for many people, despite the position of behaviorism, which is more concerned with immediate structuring for purposes of changing behavior.

Gestalt therapy will predictably continue to make an impact upon the helping professions, and it will undoubtedly experience some significant changes itself in the years ahead. The attention given to the involvement of the individual in the therapeutic process, and in his experiencing as a growth-promoting entity, has considerable merit. Waiting for awareness or for insights to occur probably has less support than ever before as a therapeutic process. The hope that with awareness will come behavior changes and better adjustment has less to support it than the idea that with experiencing a person will be more likely to abandon his systems and adopt more meaningful behaviors.

Summary

Gestalt therapy has many elements common to other theories, while still enjoying some elements of uniqueness. It is founded within the tradition of learning theory but has adopted some of the broader concepts associated with the client-centered approach, as well as some from rational-emotive therapy and reality therapy.

The concept of wholeness characterizes this theory, as the individual is seen as a unified, functioning whole. The parts have meaning only as they relate to the whole and have little meaning in isolation. Environment is also viewed as a source of great influence upon the individual, as he reacts to and acts upon the environment.

Current reality is stressed, as the total organism receives the necessary attention to bring about needed behavioral changes. Growth occurs through a reaction of the individual to his perceptual field, which is subject to change through interaction with the environment.

The concepts of "wholeness," of the perceptual field, and of interaction with the environment as a stimulator of growth are acceptable to growth counseling. However, in the latter, stress is given to the development of the internal resources of the individual as the key to his successful functioning and good adjustment. The quality of the relationship is also stressed, thus resulting in a rejection of abrupt confrontation as a therapeutic approach.

Study and discussion problems

1. Explain, as well as you can, the relationship between gestalt and learning theory.
2. Identify what you regard as perhaps the major contribution of gestalt therapy to the helping professions.
3. Move through each of the main concepts of this approach, and explain each to the satisfaction of your listeners.
4. Enumerate some of the main techniques used in this approach. Indicate which of these you feel hold the greatest promise for success.
5. React to the author's critique of the different elements in this theory.

References

Corsini, R., ed. 1973. *Current psychotherapies.* Itasca, Illinois: F. E. Peacock. Pp. 251–286.

Patterson, C. H., 2nd ed., 1973. *Theories of counseling and psychotherapy.* New York: Harper and Row. Pp. 344–377.

Perls, F., Hefferline, R., and Goodman, P. 1965. *Gestalt therapy.* New York: Dell.

Shertzer, B., and Stone, S. C. 1968, 2nd ed., 1974. *Fundamentals of counseling.* Boston: Houghton Mifflin Company. Pp. 228–233.

/ 12 /

Logotherapy

Logotherapy is a therapeutic approach with a close association with the existential philosophy designed to assist individuals with psychological problems. Frequently these problems have to do with life and its meaning, the future, success, work, and love and other human relationships. It concerns itself more with man's philosophy toward life, and his ability to deal with life, than it does with trying to determine the purpose of existence. Freedom of choice is stressed as a prerogative of the individual, but with the understanding that he is responsible for his choices and his actions (Patterson 1966).

Logotherapy is concerned about how man responds to the various circumstances and conditions of life with which he is confronted. The philosophy underlying this approach is that man must find meaning in life, and that the depth of his own being must transcend any circumstance of life that might constitute a threat to his existence or well-being.

It is designed to deal with the individual's philosophical and spiritual problems. This being the case, little consideration is given to extensive histories or to candid and uninhibited disclosures of the client's deepest thoughts and concerns. It believes that the individual in therapy can best be helped by an exploration and clarification of his value system, and by bolstering his own ego system.

Background

Logotherapy had its beginning with Viktor Frankl, who was born in Vienna, Austria, in 1905, where he continued to live and receive his education. He earned his M.D. and later his Ph.D. from the University of Vienna. A broad background of experiences in a number of clinical and medical settings contributed to his unusual competence and skill in medical practice.

The bitter and unbelievably severe experiences endured by Frankl while confined in Nazi concentration camps during World War II contributed markedly to his depth of character and to the philosophy he was able to develop. It was his contention that man must find the internal strength with which both to face and to conquer any circumstance of life, no matter how bitter. Efforts to conquer or to break him down by his Nazi captors always failed because of his ability to see himself as above and inaccessible to his tormentors. He was able to avoid a complete capitulation to despair by virtue of his belief that he was beyond the reach of those who sought to destroy him.

He was able to develop a philosophy that stressed the need to find meaning in one's existence. The discovery of meaning in life made his own existence possible under the most trying and horrendous circumstances. This same philosophy provided the framework for a therapeutic approach that has found considerable favor with psychotherapists and counselors. Its merits and value have exceeded the limits of medical practice and have contributed to educational practice and to philosophical consideration by many people throughout the world. The meaning and value found in all aspects of life make it possible for the individual to withstand and overcome any obstacle or hardship in life. Frankl has thus suggested a new dimension for living that makes sense and provides the harassed or discouraged individual with the encouragement and a pattern for living upon which he may optimistically pin his hopes and aspirations.

Man's Search for Meaning and his many other publications attest to the scholarship, imagination, and spiritual depth of Frankl. His influence perhaps knows no limits.

Major theoretical elements

Basic to logotherapy is the concept that man is capable of maintaining a sense of dignity and of spiritual freedom even under adverse circumstances. This philosophy undoubtedly had its inception with the experiences Frankl endured in the Nazi concentration camps. It is this sense of dignity characterized by an awareness of one's right to freedom that makes life meaningful and purposeful (Frankl 1962*b*). It is the ability to see purpose in life that permits man to disassociate himself from those events and conditions that would otherwise make his life miserable and even destroy him. Discomfort, unhappiness, and even suffering have a purpose in life. These conditions have a function in making life ultimately more meaningful and even more desirable.

The inability to see, to sense, and to respond to the inevitable conditions in life makes him vulnerable to the very conditions he must endure or control. Indeed, these very conditions, so frequently abhorred and resisted by man, are the means by which he can grow beyond himself. A comfortable, nonchallenging life fails to provide for the very opportunities essential to the development of spiritual and psychological strength. Therefore, pain and discomfort in some form are the inevitable prerequisites to growth. Faith in oneself and in the future makes it possible for the individual to deal with these conditions satisfactorily, and actually to profit from the experiences.

Main concepts of logotherapy

Attendant to a better understanding of logotherapy is a summarization of the main concepts it embraces. More than an orientation to the philosophical notions underlying it is thus necessary. For example, we know the idea that man must find meaning and purpose in all aspects of life is philosophically basic to this theory. We also know, however, that many interpretations of this notion are possible. How to achieve this goal is also a matter of considerable concern. To find purpose and meaning in life is no doubt quite elusive. The attainment of this condition is, however, basic to the philosophy underlying logotherapy. The idea that suffering and deprivation have a purpose, and that they really constitute opportunities for growth for the individual is also a key concept in this theory.

1. Man as a spiritual being. Although man is made up of three primary dimensions, physical, mental, and spiritual, it is the latter that constitutes the real heart of man. And while conventional psychoanalysis has given considerable attention to the first two, its neglect of the spiritual is most evident. As the chief attribute of man, spirituality prompts conscience and love (Patterson 1966).

2. Man as a free being. Man has a freedom of choice, and it is this freedom that makes possible his uniqueness and his achievements. He, alone, to a great extent, determines what he will become. Although it is recognized that man is influenced by instincts, inherited conditions, dispositions, and the environment, he still has considerable freedom to act within those conditions. Man, then, does more than just live; he has the power to give meaning to that life. He also has the power to overcome or to rise above undesirable or limiting conditions.

3. Man as a responsible being. Freedom implies the existence of avenues by which man may act and become. Freedom means more than the absence of oppressive restriction, it means that the way is open for one to progress and to achieve. Responsible action is fundamental to his existence, since such action initiates and permits freedom. He has a responsibility first to himself as a condition of gratitude for existence, and second to others because of his dependence upon others for a meaningful existence.

Man is, then, very much a social being who stands in need of the opportunity to influence and to be influenced by others. It is from others that he gains the necessary stimulation and encouragement through which his greatest potential may be achieved. He likewise needs the opportunity to share himself with others, since it is through this sharing that he profits.

4. Man is motivated by a will to meaning. The motivation underlying man's genuine efforts toward a fruitful life is the will to meaning. The intense, intrinsic desire to find meaning in life provides the fire for action. An absence of such a desire, or an attitude of complete indifference to life, is what Frankl (1962a) calls "the existential vacuum." The consequent void of such a state of inner emptiness serves as a serious challenge to psychiatry. It is through man's efforts to overcome this void that he gains the necessary internal strength that underlies his own meaningful and fruitful actions.

5. Man as an unmotivated being. Much of man's difficulties rest with his inability to find meaning in life. An inner emptiness characterizes his existence and contributes to his feelings of worthlessness. An existential vacuum (Frankl 1962a) persists, resulting in extreme boredom, uncertainty, and confusion. Although this condition is one of spiritual distress, it is not necessarily a mental disease. It is this distress that gives man his greatest concern and constitutes a most serious deterrent to his happiness and to his effectiveness.

With sufficient motivation, a man will search and strive for meaning in life, and he will find the answers to his great need for activity and productivity. Such a search may increase rather than reduce tension, but this is good since mental health depends upon an appropriate level of tension. The effort to reduce the gap between what one would like to become and what one perceives himself as being is gradually reduced through a response to tension.

6. Man as neurotic or psychotic. Existential conflict or frustration exists to some degree in most individuals. In this case, he is neither neurotic nor psychotic, but he is experiencing some difficulties. If he is unable to see meaning and purpose in life, and thus overcome his frustration, a neurotic or psychotic state may be the result.

The key to good mental health and to a purposeful life is found in man's ability to anticipate and live his life with zest and with meaningful action. It is through useful activity, commitment to a purpose, and meaningful relationships with others that man is able to see a purpose to life. It is by virtue of the spiritual strength he develops that he is able to live profitably and meaningfully.

Techniques of logotherapy

Logos has a twofold meaning, in that logos refers to "meaning," but it also means "spiritual." The therapeutic process, then, must be directed toward the existential and the spiritual nature of man. This concept immediately suggests a therapeutic approach that is broad, philosophically oriented, and flexible. In other words, it does not subscribe to any one set of techniques, but rather concerns itself with the philosophical, psychological, and spiritual aspects of one's being. Man is viewed as a whole, with considerable emphasis upon the spiritual, thus the focus upon meanings in life and upon the values of the individual.

Diagnosis is used for purposes of determining whether the causes of the difficulties are essentially physical, psychological, or spiritual. It is assumed that each has a part in the emotional disturbance and that diagnosis will help in clarifying the place of each. If a physical factor is the primary cause, medication is in order for treatment. The term most appropriately used is "psychosis." If a psychological factor is primary, the term "noögenic neurosis" is normally used (Patterson 1966). The latter occurs from a conflict of values.

Since the aim of logotherapy is a greater sense of responsibility by the individual for himself, the techniques most likely to accomplish this goal are used. Teaching, directing, and guiding are techniques utilized in achieving the goal. However, any technique used is subject to the therapist's desire to develop a good working relationship. Problems and concerns are discussed frankly, but without preaching, moralizing, or arguing.

Cases of high anxiety and obsessive-compulsive neuroses lend themselves to two therapeutic techniques. Anxiety neuroses and phobic conditions are characterized by anticipatory anxiety, which leads to a condition engendering even greater anxiety. Thus begins a vicious cycle that must be broken if the individual is to overcome his anxieties. This is accomplished through a technique described by Frankl (1960) as paradoxical intention.

Anticipatory anxiety is the term used by Frankl to describe what happens to a fearful individual. Fearing or anticipating an event actually brings the event to pass. In other words, a fear-evoking situation is anticipated with intense anxiety, and when it actually occurs, the individual is, indeed, very fearful and very anxious. This cycle is broken through the use of paradoxical intention. This involves having the individual make a conscious effort to get worse or to call up the fear that has been giving the difficulty. For example, if he has an intense fear of riding in an elevator and is fearful of passing out with fear, he deliberately puts himself into this situation and tries to pass out. The repeated use of this technique with persistence and patience will frequently bring a complete relief from the earlier symptoms.

Dereflection is another technique that consists of ignoring the trouble. In this case the individual's awareness is directed toward the positive aspects of a situation. He must be redirected from his anticipatory anxiety to something more appealing. Dereflection thus contributes to the individual's ability to ignore his neurosis by removing the focus upon himself to something outside of self. The idea here is to get the individual interested in a life full of potential meanings with strong personal appeal (Frankl 1960).

A critique of logotherapy

Finding something about which to quarrel within logotherapy may be difficult since so many of its precepts make good sense. What it has to offer, then, is highly palatable and even exciting. Its biggest problem may well rest with its oversimplification of the nature of the human personality, and with the assumption that most individuals have the capacity to develop a spiritual depth upon which they can truly depend. Its major weakness may then lie in an optimism about man that is not wholly justified. If everyone could find a true and deep meaning for his existence and if he could attain a level of deep spiritual significance, then logotherapy could be the ultimate in man's search for relevance. Unfortunately, the attainment of such attitudes is so elusive as to make the whole theory somewhat vulnerable.

A response to logotherapy

The growth-counseling concept emphasizes the reality of man and of the world. Although it stresses and strives for the development of spiritual depth in man, it takes a realistic view as to the possibilities for doing so. Greater stress is given to the notion that most people can be helped in developing a greater internal strength upon which they can depend in time of stress. The very act of developing this internal strength also has merit as the actions involved and the intellectual and emotional commitments included are meshed in a meaningful engagement that is both invigorating and potentially beneficial.

The notion that one must find meaning in life and that even suffering has a purpose is a meaningful and exciting one. How to get the despondent, the discouraged, the ill, and the indifferent individuals to achieve this lofty goal is a formidable problem. Not all people have the courage, the spirit, or the willing attitude essential to such a realization, nor is everyone able to gain the needed emotional insight leading to a positive and accepting attitude toward all aspects of life. Logotherapy may, then, be regarded as philosophically sound, but as quite vulnerable to the onslaught of reality.

It may be true, for example, that man is capable of maintaining a sense of dignity and freedom under adverse conditions, but realizing this capability to even a minimal level is another matter. It is likewise true that man should possess the ability to see purpose in life, but really doing so is a rarity. Creditable indeed is the notion that even suffering and hardships have a purpose, and that man can profit from these experiences. In truth, however, most individuals vehemently resist any condition that forebodingly promises pain. They not only fail to see the merit in discomfort but also actively seek pleasure and comfort. They are inclined to take any necessary chances to avoid pain and disavow the notion that it holds a promise for personal growth and meaning.

How does one truly reach the point at which he is able to see meaning in all aspects of life? By what philosophical route or therapeutic process might this be achieved? Or, might we conclude that this is an unrealistic goal, and that a more logical position includes the view that man is not likely to change so drastically as to become the kind of individual that Frankl so hopefully describes?

1. Man as a spiritual being. Man is indeed a spiritual as well as a physical and psychological being. But how well does he know this, and how receptive is he to the notion? Growth counseling takes the view that the spiritual (although nonreligious) is only a vaguely perceived concept for most men, rendering it relatively ineffective as a source of inspiration or action. The concept of spirituality is not enough to make up the internal core of the individual. It is only a part of what we are identifying as an internal strength upon which the individual can depend, and from which he can draw in making needed adjustments and adaptions.

There is a need, then, to provide for a variety of growth-promoting experiences during the growing years of the individual. Appropriate experiences are also essential to the continuing growth and progress of the individual throughout his adult years. It is through such activities that attitudes are formed, character is built, and skills are developed. It is upon a framework of self-confidence, social and technical skills, and academic competence that the individual is able to continually build and increase his strengths and magnify his capacities.

2. Man as a free being. The essentiality of freedom, as described in logotherapy, is in fact basic to man's good and welfare. His freedom to choose does add to his uniqueness and to his sense of dignity. However, desirable as the concept of freedom is, the choice to act is frequently the undoing of many individuals. Growth counseling does not suggest that he be denied this freedom, but rather it stresses that the freedom to act is merely a condition for which man needs to be prepared. Growth counseling, then, does not deny freedom, but it does assume considerable responsibility for helping individuals learn how to use it and how to live with the outcomes of their choices.

Growth counseling maintains that a denial or a postponement of acting is often essential in order to help some individuals protect themselves against choices that may later lead to regrets. In other words, the emotion of a situation or the desperation of the person may prompt an act that may be illogical and fraught with unpleasant outcomes. It is the function of the counselor to work closely with the individual, to explore alternatives, and to make decisions upon the basis of facts and conditions.

3. Man as a responsible being. The position that man is or might be a responsible individual is a sound one. The test lies in determining how to get him to this state, or what to do with him if he proves to be irresponsible. Through freedom, man is able to express himself, to achieve, and to produce. This same freedom suggests the need for a deep sense of personal responsibility. Its need is thus evident to the counselor, whose efforts are directed toward teaching and helping the individual toward an ever-increasing sense of responsibility.

The recognition of man as a social being in need of opportunities for interaction with others is immediately acceptable. The counselor's approaches and relationships with the client constantly reflect this attitude. Again, this notion must be carried beyond the philosophical stage and made applicable. One of the realitites of growth counseling is the dimension that unhesitatingly provides opportunities for the client to try out and to apply his new learnings. The mere articulation of a theoretical notion is not enough.

4. Man is motivated by a will to meaning. The belief that man is motivated by a will to meaning has surface merit, but it fails to provide for those who have lost or who have failed to develop a will to meaning. We see counseling as a reinforcing, encouraging, stimulating element in one's life from which some insights toward the meaningfulness of life may be gained. Opportunity for action is also essential here, as it is through involvement with others and through the manipulation of ideas, translated into movement, that man ultimately sees the true meaning in life.

The existential vacuum probably exists to a degree in most people. The challenge to the counselor is one of avoiding such a condition, through the encouragement of action and involvement for his client, or at least its minimization. Growth counseling does not accept the notion that this inner emptiness is an inevitable condition, or that it cannot be overcome by virtually all individuals. Even the individual with a limited mentality can be helped to appreciate the beauties, challenges, and merits of life. Appropriate experiences are needed as the essentials for the attainment of positive attitudes and for a zestful pursuit of life's activities.

5. Man as an unmotivated being. Man may indeed be characterized by a lack of motivation, but this condition need not continue for the individual. There are ways through which he can be helped to see and to feel the keen and stimulating elements of a highly motivated life. This is where the counselor's effectivenees is put to the test. To help an unmotivated individual become sufficiently motivated as to increase his productive output and to better his enthusiasm for life constitutes a real challenge. This can be accomplished, however, by the skilled, concerned counselor whose genuineness is sensed by the client and whose ability to be of real help becomes evident.

As the client comes to sense the genuine concern of the counselor, and as he gains an appreciation for the counselor, his own resources for more vigorous, meaningful action may be more fully utilized. Perhaps no condition does more for the motivation of an individual than one characterized by a deep, genuine caring by a responsible counselor. It is the knowledge and awareness of this caring that trigger an emotional response in the individual leading to fruitful, determined action.

6. Man as neurotic or psychotic. Man need be neither neurotic nor psychotic. An admission to this condition is essentially an indictment against society, and most uncomplimentary to the individual. Although it is no doubt true that existential conflict or frustration exists to some degree in most individuals, such conflict need not be tolerated or seen as inevitable. The fact that many individuals fail to see meaning and purpose in life, as Frankl has indicated, need not persist as a permanent circumstance. A condition becomes inevitable only to the degree to which the individual permits it to become so. Growth counseling stresses the development and utilization of one's internal resources and the full exploration of the environment.

Efforts toward the achievement of this goal leave little time or space for the development of symptoms of neurosis or psychosis. It is through productive and zestful involvement in exciting activities, and through interaction with others, that the individual recognizes and feels a real purpose in life. All neurotic or psychotic tendencies are not necessarily eliminated even under ideal conditions of activity and involvement, but they can certainly be minimized through appropriate counseling and teaching approaches.

The future of logotherapy

The concepts of logotherapy are educationally and therapeutically promising and can be expected to continue to make an impact upon many of the helping professions. The philosophy underlying logotherapy also has a certain appeal, and the logical, common-sense elements included are popular with many people.

The notion that one must find meaning and purpose in life if he is to function effectively and experience happiness provides an optimistic guideline for many people. This notion suggests that life does indeed have meaning and that it can be found by anyone who actively pursues it. These and other ideas espoused by logotherapy provide a philosophical framework within which most people can function satisfactorily.

The limitations of this therapy are not too different from those encountered in other therapies that depend heavily upon philosophy. It is relatively easy to say how man should feel and behave, but quite another matter to get him to the point at which this ideal will be achieved. Additional time and the efforts of concerned therapists may provide some additional answers to the yet unanswered questions concerning the best techniques for effecting significant changes in man's behavior.

Summary

Logotherapy is a therapeutic approach markedly influenced by an existential philosophy, and it is designed to assist individuals with psychological problems. It has a philosophic consideration for the meaning of life to man and stresses the necessity of man's seeing purpose in life.

This therapy had its beginning with Victor Frankl, who earned his M.D. and Ph.D. degrees from the University of Vienna. His experiences as a prisoner of the Nazis in concentration camps during World War II provided the background for the philosophy underlying this theory.

The concept basic to logotherapy is that man has the capacity to maintain a sense of dignity and personal freedom even under the most adverse circumstances. Suffering and hardship have a purpose, and man can profit from this realization.

Man is viewed as a spiritual, free, and responsible individual who has the ability to maintain a kind of aloofness that makes him less vulnerable to the realities of a harsh world. Man must find meaning in life, and it is this meaning that motivates him toward a productive life. Any tendency toward low motivation must be overcome through seeing meaning in life and in living purposefully. A failure to experience life as meaningful may lead to neurotic or psychotic conditions.

The techniques used in logotherapy are marked by flexibility and experimentation. The idea is to accommodate the person, rather than to observe a particular technique. Paradoxical intention and dereflection are frequently used.

Logotherapy will likely continue to have a great influence upon counseling and psychotherapy despite its fairly obvious limitations. It may indeed be beneficial for man to view himself as a spiritual being and for him to find meaning in life. How to help him achieve this attitude or condition is the challenge.

Growth counseling stresses the utilization of experiences and the involvement of the individual in growth-promoting activities through which he will gain needed insights. He is likewise taught or exposed to ideas from which may come insights and needed behavioral changes.

Growth counseling is not content with what should be, but rather concentrates upon the person as a growing individual with the capacities to continue to enhance himself with each passing day.

Study and discussion problems

1. Explain the meaning of the term *logotherapy*. Discuss the appropriateness of this term to the concepts of the theory.
2. Explain as well as you can the relationship between Frankl as a person, including his experiences, and the philosophy underlying this theory.
3. Summarize and criticize each of the main concepts of this theory in your own words.
4. If you had the task of extending this theory to concepts not now included, explain what you would like to include.

References

Frankl, V. E. 1962. *Man's search for meaning.* Boston: Beacon Press.
Patterson, C. H. 1966, 2nd ed., 1973. *Theories of counseling and psychotherapy.* New York: Harper and Row. Pp. 428–456.

/ 13 /

Existentialism in counseling and psychotherapy

Many of the current theories claim a background in the traditional psychoanalytic or behavioristic approaches. Existentialism is regarded as something of a third force in psychology, and as a contribution of philosophical thought. This being the case, it is not normally regarded as a counseling or as a therapeutic approach as is the case with the other theories covered in this book. It is rather viewed as a philosophy, the understanding and application of which have made a significant impact upon counseling and psychotherapy.

Existentialism has been more concerned with the presuppositions underlying therapy than it has with any system of techniques (Ford and Urban 1963). The assumptions about the nature of man, then, provide some notions for therapeutic techniques, but they do not prescribe the techniques. The first assumption tells us that man has the capacity for an awareness of self and of his surroundings. This awareness makes possible responsible action and decisions. Another assumption is that behavior has meaning only as it is seen in the context of the event toward which the behavior is directed. A third assumption notes the need for a phenomenological research method as a means for gaining scientific knowledge, since the procedures of natural science are not appropriate.

There has been, then, a dependence upon existentialism for ideas that give depth, meaning, and purpose to the therapeutic process.

Background

Just as psychoanalytic theory has a history in the late nineteenth and early twentieth century, so, too, does existentialism. Thought preliminary to existentialism actually predated Freud and the psychoanalytic theory, however, as various philosophies and points of view were being developed and considered. Some vagueness has characterized existentialism, and perhaps even mysticism, as difficulties have been encountered in defining and classifying it. In reality, existentialism has included elements of theology, philosophy, psychiatry, and psychology, with a goal of a better understanding of human behavior (Shertzer and Stone 1968).

Existentialism is the outcome of considerable in-depth thinking on the part of a number of individuals with a vital concern in the nature of man. The names of a few individuals are most prominent here: Sören Kierkegaard, Paul Tillich, Jean Paul Sartre, Rollo May, Erich Fromm, and others. Although these men differed on some points, their views coincided with the basic concepts of the philosophy. Victor Frankl is often placed in this camp since his logotherapy incorporates many of the same views as existentialism.

Existentialism has had a philosophical impact upon counseling and psychotherapy over the years because of its kinship with psychotherapy in its attempt to explain behavior and to find remedies for maladjustments. It has permeated many of the psychotherapeutic approaches, particularly as it has attempted to bring meaning to these approaches.

Major theoretical elements

The fundamental basis of existentialism is an attempt to understand an individual as he really is within his reality, and to see and understand his world as he sees it (May, et al. 1958). This notion has particular significance for the counselor, as he sees the merit in understanding the needs of the individual and for the individual to come to a better understanding of himself. Since counseling is essentially a process of helping the individual toward freedom, and a humanizing of the person who has lost his freedom (van Kaam 1962), we can see the importance of any philosophy that adds to man's dignity. The person who has become dehumanized is aided toward regaining his freedoms by helping him gain insights into the meaning of the situations that have created a threat to him. The extinction of inappropriate responses and the conditioning of desirable behaviors are also accomplished.

Man is central to all meaningful existence in the world. His constant strivings to become are a reflection of his need for feelings of importance and for status. The world should make adjustments to accommodate man, rather than forcing him to have to change to meet the fickle expectations of others. The vagueness that constitutes man himself and the lack of clarity within the world make it necessary for man to give first and careful consideration to his own welfare.

Main concepts of existentialism

Perhaps even the best informed individuals experience some difficulty in attempting a precise description of this philosophy. Even those concepts that are frequently identified are subject to a variety of interpretations. The elimination of personal impressions and the attainment of objectivity in describing highly philosophical and largely intangible concepts are essentially impossible. The following topics thus represent only an attempt to highlight some of the major beliefs of this philosophy.

1. Man as a meaningful whole. Existentialism views man as a meaningful whole who is constantly in a state of being and in the process of becoming. An understanding of man in depth thus remains as a constant goal of existentialism, and it is not content with the relatively superficial knowledge of man normally available. It attempts to go beyond the surface, the obvious, in order to achieve a knowledge of man from which help toward greater accomplishments might be realized.

Man is characterized as both being and becoming. "Being" is an awareness of self, how he views self, and what he makes of himself. "Becoming" suggests a constant striving toward improvements.

2. Emotionality and adjustment. An understanding of existentialism requires an acceptance of anxiety and of guilt as central to that understanding. Anxiety in this case is the experience of a threat of imminent nonbeing (May, et al. 1958). In striving toward fulfillment, the individual experiences anxiety, probably because of a fear of failure. Feelings of guilt are his lot if he denies his potentiality or if he fails to measure up. Anxiety and guilt are thus key elements in the emotionality of the individual and in his adjustment. The reduction of anxiety through the successful pursuit of becoming something important appears necessary. Guilt must likewise be reduced by making the most of one's opportunities for becoming.

3. Time and adjustment. Time has meaning for the individual, but not in the conventional sense. Since man is constantly in the process of becoming, it is not possible to define him at any one point in time. The changes he is making within himself, or is instrumental in achieving, result in his being a somewhat different person at one point in time than at another. It is to the individual's advantage to repress certain experiences from the past about which he may otherwise feel guilty. Although he is never completely free from the past, he avoids the burdens imposed by it through looking to the future. A failure to anticipate the promises of the future may contribute to neuroticism, while a healthy expectation of the future motivates the individual to distinctive action.

4. Transcending the present. The ability of man to transcend the present, and to anticipate the future, constitutes a unique quality upon which he can capitalize. Going beyond the present thus makes it possible for him to contemplate what he would like to become, and what he would like to gain from the future.

5. The application of freedom. Freedom is an important notion here, as man is seen as having a choice and as following his own dictates. Many existentialists see man as the determiner of his culture, and not as its victim. Determinism is not rejected as a real element in the world, but neither is it accepted as having direct application to man. He lives within the laws of his culture, but he controls or transcends them, rather than being controlled (Arbuckle 1965). The circumstances of life exercise some influence over man, and he is never completely free of them. However, he is still free to act within these existing conditions. He is in control, not the environment.

6. Man as a responsible creature. The precise nature of man includes concepts that emphasize the responsibility of man for his acts. The thirteen propositions outlined by Beck (1963) all focus upon the concept of responsibility. Under these propositions, man has the responsibility to:

1. be responsible for his acts and face the reality of existing unchangeable conditions;
2. aid others and act kindly toward others;
3. base decisions upon the effect they may have upon mankind and exercise one's freedom of choice within this structure;
4. counsel others and be counseled by others in order to meet life's problems;
5. operate somewhat independently since he has no knowledge of a supernatural creation; and
6. avoid suffering for himself and others by learning from the experiences of others and by aiding less fortunate individuals.

Therapeutic techniques

Since existentialism is a philosophy or a point of view and not a precise counseling or therapeutic approach, there is little to be said about the techniques utilized. The techniques used obviously are in keeping with the viewpoint of existentialism. It should also be noted that there are various viewpoints even within the structure of existentialism, thus resulting in a variety of techniques used by therapists.

There is, however, a kinship between existentialism and client-centered counseling, which dictates to a degree the techniques used. The reflection of feelings within an atmosphere characterized by warmth and understanding is a core technique. The counselor is accepting and permissive, and he encourages a candid expression of feelings and emotions.

Some of the more directive and confrontation counseling approaches are also possible under the existential philosophy. It does not attempt to dictate techniques, but rather to provide a philosophical explanation for the nature and importance of man. The attitudes of the individual counselor toward man, and his convictions about the relative merits and quality of man, influence him as a counselor and dictate to a degree the approaches he uses to help an individual resolve his problems and plan for the future.

A critique of existentialism

The possible merits of existentialism are perhaps fairly obvious to most counselors and psychotherapists. There is probably little with which to quarrel in the viewpoints presented. For example, the idea of attempting to come to a better understanding of man is a valuable and commendable one. The concepts of stressing the importance of the individual, and of his exercising considerable freedom in the control of his own destiny, are also commendable elements.

The need to experience feelings of importance is essentially universal, and any system that recognizes this and attempts to help the individual achieve these feelings should be enthusiastically welcomed. The centrality of man to all meaningful existence provides for a sense of dignity and of hope for the future, which cannot logically be denied.

A response to existentialism

A critique of existentialism should more logically focus upon certain beliefs that appear open to question, rather than the philosophy as a whole. Since there are disagreements among existentialists, and varying degrees of emphasis placed upon the different beliefs, the attempt toward a critical analysis is difficult and perhaps even impossible.

1. Man as a meaningful whole. Man is, indeed, a meaningful whole, but growth counseling views the quality of man as being determined by his significant relationships with others and his power in influencing others toward a better life. It is also true that man is constantly in the process of becoming; however, growth counseling feels the need to provide considerable direction in assessing and developing capacities and in helping the individual decide what it is he wants to become. Goal establishment is essential here, and it is followed with some structured procedures for attaining a goal.

An awareness of self is viewed as a condition that facilitates realistic self-assessment and provides direction for continuing growth and personal improvements. "Becoming" is viewed less as a distant goal and more as an emphasis upon rich, exciting, meaningful living in the present. Activity and involvement in many growth-promoting endeavors are stressed.

2. Emotionality and adjustment. Anxiety and guilt are viewed in growth counseling as conditions that are inevitable. The nature of the human personality, combined with the unavoidable vicissitudes of life, creates a situation in which there is no complete escape from the anxieties that precede real or imaginary events or from the guilt that follows failures. The avoidance of anxieties is stressed through helping the individual prepare for the anticipated events of the future, thus reducing the logical occurrence of anxiety. Considerable attention is also given to developing self-confidence and bolstering self-esteem as preludes to handling potentially anxiety-evoking situations.

Intelligent planning and decision making are also stressed with the belief that key decisions will reduce the possibilities for anxieties and for guilt feelings. Since guilt occurs from a person's doing or failing to do something that is important to him, it can be avoided by doing what should be done and avoiding mistakes. The guilt that comes to many people because of failures to fulfill their potential need not occur, and ideally under the growth-counseling concept, guilt will be of minimal influence if it does occur. The individual is given direction and encouragement and the opportunities for fulfillment, and he is helped toward successful achievements, thus reducing the possibilities for any guilt feelings.

3. Time and adjustment. Although man may have the capacity to transcend the present and to be constantly changing, growth counseling views time as merely a condition of the world, not to be given undue attention. The movement of time is one of the inevitabilities of the universe, and a condition to be accepted without elation or dismay. The critical points here are how man uses his time as it becomes available to him and with how much seriousness he anticipates and prepares for the future. He has no need to regret the past or dread the future if he has made the most of the past and is able to welcome enthusiastically the offerings of the future.

The individual is not disturbed by the thoughts of an unproductive or uninviting future because he has learned to trust time and to develop confidence in himself and in his ability to cope with occurring events. Growth counseling stresses the importance of the individual as a permanent occupant of the universe, with no limitation upon his ultimate achievements, except as limited by his own attitudes.

4. Transcending the present. To transcend the present and look to the future has merit only to the degree to which it results in more fully living the present. Growth counseling deplores any suggestion that implies an abandonment of the present in an overzealous searching for the future. Instead, emphasis should be given to the most productive and effective living possible today, and this in and of itself is the best possible preparation for the future. The striving to become is, in reality, an effective utilization of the present, with an optimistic outlook to the future.

5. The application of freedom. Freedom is, of course, a concept against which we can wage no argument, although there are many interpretations of the term. To have the prerogative of choice in actions and to follow one's own dictates are obviously meaningful and cherished conditions for most men. Likewise, men should have considerable control over the culture and be its master, not its victim.

Growth counseling sees freedom as a condition in which man

functions widely, creatively, and imaginatively, but within a structure that abides by the rules of logic and good judgment. Any action that jeopardizes the welfare of the behaver or any other individual is in reality a violation of freedom. Growth counseling also sees man as moral, which simply means that his behavior is consistently within the limits of societal expectations, personal logic, and the best interests of others.

6. Man as a responsible creature. The responsibility of man as a social creature is a well-accepted notion. His obligation to consider the welfare of others in attempting to fulfill his own needs is fundamental to responsible citizenship in a society. Man's responsibility to assist others is essentially acceptable.

There is an element of the ideal in this position, however, and little help is given in pointing out how man is to be brought to this level of mature concern for others. Growth counseling maintains that this ideal position is attained to the degree to which the individual sees himself (self-concept) as a competent, worthy, important individual. He considers others and helps others, if such behavior brings him satisfaction and carries no threat to his position. If he perceives his associations with others as inviting a situation with possibilities for threat, he will resist such associations. So the problem is one of building strength and self-confidence in the individual to the point at which he sees others as sources of satisfaction and not as threats to his own position.

The future of existentialism

The work of the existentialists has been of such quality and has held such universal appeal that the continuation and expansion of existentialism are certainly assured. The changing philosophies of the times that continue to place greater stress upon the importance of man in the universe likewise promise new and exciting ideas.

Existentialism also provides for a philosophical structure that lends meaning and coherence to many of the counseling theories. This condition adds to the status and prestige of existentialism as its importance to counseling theory is recognized and utilized. It is conceivable, then, that these theories will need to define their positions in the future in terms of the existential concepts. An acceptance of these concepts may predictably add strength and meaning to all counseling and psychotherapy theories of the future.

Summary

Existentialism is essentially a philosophy with certain assumptions that have relevance to the therapeutic process. These assumptions have been useful in developing counseling techniques and in coming to a better understanding of the human personality. This striving to understand an individual within the reality of his situation is basic to existentialism.

Man is seen as a meaningful whole who is constantly in the process of becoming. Anxiety and guilt are inevitable outcomes of these strivings. Time is meaningful only in the context of what is happening to the individual at a particular time.

The anticipation of a more promising future persists as man views himself as constantly changing and improving. This anticipation is made more meaningful by the stress given to freedom as a condition essential to man's destiny. Responsibility is very much a part of this freedom.

Existentialism is viewed as a very influential force in counseling and psychotherapy. Its limitations are seen in its undue emphasis upon the future and its preoccupation with anxiety and guilt as possible deterrents to progress. Growth counseling stresses more particularly meaningful living today as an adequate and desirable preparation for the future. The notion of freedom within an arbitrary structure of limitations is a reality of the times. The responsibility of man not only to make the most of his opportunities but also actually to create opportunities for himself is also stressed.

Study and discussion problems

1. Identify what you regard as the greatest contributions of existentialism to counseling and psychotherapy.

2. Describe in your own terminology what you see as the heart of existentialism.
3. In what ways should a philosophy contribute to a counseling approach? What should the results be?
4. Enumerate and react to each of the main concepts of existentialism.
5. Describe the counseling approaches of the counselor who subscribes to existentialism.
6. Make a brief critical analysis of existentialism in terms of your own beliefs concerning the nature of man.

References

Corsini, R., ed. 1973. *Current psychotherapies.* Itasca, Illinois: F. E. Peacock. Pp. 317–352.

Ford, D. H., and Urban, H. B. 1965. *Systems of psychotherapy.* New York: John Wiley and Sons. Pp. 445–480.

Shertzer, B., and Stone, S. C. 1968, 2nd ed., 1974. *Fundamentals of counseling.* Boston: Houghton Mifflin Company. Pp. 223–228.

/ 14 /

Growth counseling as a contributor to counseling theory

Each of the main counseling theories has been summarized and criticized in the chapters of this text. The summarizations have provided the key concepts of each theory. The reader should now have a better feeling for each theory, in addition to having acquired some information about each. The critiques have helped identify some of the possible limitations of each theory and have provided information as to the needed ingredients in a counseling theory.

Growth counseling has been used as a title for a kind of counseling that incorporates many elements of current theories into a meaningful and practical counseling approach. It also suggests a philosophy that makes possible a counseling approach with more innovative possibilities than the current theories offer. Growth counseling utilizes the best of present theories, while still extending the concepts beyond the framework of each existing theory. It places considerable stress upon the development of the individual's internal resources as a source of strength and direction in resolving problems and capitalizing upon opportunities.

The logic of a better theory

Commendable as many of the concepts and elements of the present theories may be, there is still a need for a counseling theory that will better satisfy the needs of the times. So it is not a case of abandoning all current theories, but rather one of developing a theory that appropriately utilizes the best from each theory in creating a sounder and more logical approach for providing realistic and acceptable assistance for everyone, no matter what his state of adjustment or maladjustment might be. A central philosophical point of growth counseling, then, is that all individuals of every age group, and with problems of varying severity, may logically profit from the counseling experience. This philosophy also permits and stresses the use of many techniques and devices under this counseling approach, many of which are innovative and imaginative. In many cases, there is neither the time nor the need for full researching of each technique. Hopefully, research will follow and data will be gained from which changes and improvements will be made.

The need for a better theory

Fortunately, no theory is regarded as a stopping point by most competent counselors and psychotherapists. It provides some structure from which to function, and it gives philosophical direction to the counselor's ideas. It must, in reality, be a dynamic, ever-changing power in the life of the counselor, always serving as his tool and helper, never as his master. The need for changes in current theories is thus quite evident, and equally important is the need for the initiation of innovative, even radical, ideas from which newer and better theories may emerge.

The rapid and often questionable departure from tradition in our society has magnified the need for a counseling approach that may meaningfully and effectively provide direction for everyone within a variety of philosophical, ethical, and political persuasions. This notion, of course, stresses the need for the individualization of approach, and for a counselor sufficiently skilled to meet the needs of each individual, and that becomes the challenge.

A base of commonalities

The well-intentioned and yet frustrating and inefficient efforts of many counselors to bridge the gaps among the various theories may be reduced significantly by observing some relatively simple guidelines. These are designed to provide a common base from which to function, with exciting possibilities for theory reform and innovation. Such commonalities may constitute the structure for a counseling theory that hopefully serves the purposes of most counselors and meets the needs of most clients.

1. Objectives or goals. The first of these common elements is one of establishing and working toward a particular objective or goal in each counseling session. In this case, both counselor and client have a commitment to this condition and function accordingly. This approach permits considerable flexibility in techniques and allows for personality characteristics and other personal considerations. The only requirement is that a goal be established for each session, and that both client and counselor work toward its realization. Related to this expectation is one that presumes the establishment of long-term goals as a part of therapy.

An example of a goal for first and second sessions may be stated as a performance or behavioral objective.

Objective: To describe precisely the nature of the problem.

Objective: To demonstrate the ability to identify some alternative courses of action.

An example of a long-term therapeutic goal may be stated as follows:

Objective: To demonstrate the ability to give at least three five-minute talks before an audience without undue anxiety or stress.

The acceptance of the notion that there must be an established goal or objective becomes a reality for the counselor and client. This provides direction and structure and adds to the efficient use of time.

2. Principles. The establishment of and adherence to a principle give the counseling encounter meaningful direction for problem resolution and planning. This approach minimizes the vagueness and floundering that may otherwise characterize counseling. So, instead of moving directly to the use of some technique in an effort to help the individual, the counselor gives first consideration to some sound principles, which dictate to a degree the appropriateness of a technique.

Some principles appropriate to all counseling approaches, or to an integrated approach, might include the following.

a) Always view each problem revealed from the viewpoint of the client. Attempt to perceive the total situation from the perspective of the individual.

b) Create a nonjudgmental atmosphere in which the person is encouraged to express himself with candor and freedom. Minimize any possibility of his thinking that the counselor will judge or punish behavior.

c) View each individual as a whole, or as a totality of personality traits and characteristics. Realize that the isolation and treatment of a single symptom is likely to be unproductive in terms of total growth. Wholeness is essential here.

d) Avoid the temptation to focus upon a particular behavior, personality trait, or problem as if the resolution of a particular difficulty were the answer to the person's needs. Anticipate the existence of underlying conditions with a relationship to the main problems, and assume a condition of interrelationships among personality traits and among the causes of difficulties.

e) Always direct efforts toward helping the individual identify and fulfill his needs. Assume that progress toward need fulfillment will also result in the resolution of many of an individual's problems.

f) Proceed as if the best solutions to a person's problems are to be found within himself. It is the internal strength of the individual upon which he can rely most confidently for answers to his problems.

g). Demonstrate a belief in the individual from which he may gain added confidence and through which appropriate actions may be triggered. Help him to see a justification for the confidence shown in him by believing in him and by reinforcing his efforts.

h) Continually emphasize an attitude of high regard for him as a worthy human being. Help him to see his importance as a unique, deserving human being.

i) Demonstrate enthusiasm and optimism in the relationship, and help him to see the humor as well as the seriousness of his situation. A hopeful, cheerful, optimistic attitude should be a prerequisite to a concerted attack upon existing problems.

j) Focus all efforts upon strengthening and building up the individual. It is upon the increasing strength and capacities of the individual that he will be able to depend for actions and judgments.

k) Structure each counseling session in such a fashion as to identify possibilities for developing and improving needed skills. Greater competence adds to self-confidence and attracts the kind of attention that continues to bolster self-esteem.

l) Continually emphasize the notions that counseling is a shared and a sharing relationship and that all decisions are mutually achieved. Help him to feel that the tone and the quality of the relationship are a source of encouragement upon which he may draw indefinitely.

Obviously, there are other principles, but these are basic to growth counseling and are representative of the commonalities to be established in all counseling. The precise nature or number of principles is not important; however, the concept of observing principles for the improvement of counseling is most important.

3. Concepts. It is possible to identify and summarize key concepts for each theory. Once this has been done, one's familiarity with and understanding of the theory are increased considerably. It is at this point that a feeling for or about a theory may be developed. An understanding of a theory thus includes feelings, or an emotional reaction, as well as an intellectual comprehension.

These concepts constitute the heart of a theory. It is upon such concepts that a determination of techniques to be used may be made. There is a need for a set of common concepts that might logically constitute core concepts for most counseling. Such concepts are discussed in the next section of this chapter and constitute the heart of growth counseling.

The nature of growth counseling

The philosophies and points of view underlying growth counseling have been expressed throughout the critique sections dealing with each of the main theories. Statements were made as to the position of the growth-counseling concept on each of the points reviewed in the various theories. We now move to a summarization of the main concepts of growth counseling.

The concept of growth counseling

Growth counseling utilizes the individual's developmental processes and potentialities for building self-confidence, developing self-esteem, and creating an affirmative self-image. It goes beyond the assessment of the current developmental level of the individual as it seeks to maximize these developmental processes, and thus initiate an advantage for the individual. A determination of a person's current level of capabilities is done informally and somewhat incidentally, and only as a first step toward a goal of increasing and improving these capabilities.

The assessment of potentialities is done for purposes of designing experiences through which these potentialities may be improved upon and strengthened as a step toward greater productivity, resourcefulness, and imagination. The development of potentialities well beyond the level normally anticipated by the individual and his peers is an immediate goal of growth counseling. Additional goals include constantly increasing self-confidence and a positive attitude of self-assurance and faith in oneself. Long-term goals include the development of a keen sense of personal pride, the strengthening of an attitude of personal responsibility, and the attainment of high level achievements in all areas of selected endeavors.

Growth counseling encourages appropriate behavior changes essential to the full utilization and development of the individual's potentialities. It also provides for the maximum use of the environment in conjunction with the existing and developing growth process of the individual. The school setting should thus provide for an enriching, stimulating, and challenging environment in which the individual has exciting, exhilarating, and satisfying encounters with that environment.

The reduction or elimination of anxieties and frustrations remains as a constant goal of counseling. This is accomplished, in part, through the building of self-confidence and the reduction of inappropriate inhibitions. Behaviors appropriate for satisfying the individual's needs, and in keeping with society's expectations, are identified and reinforced.

A commitment to maximum personal growth and high achievement characterizes the individual's conduct as he profits from counseling, and as he begins to realize the thrilling possibilities open to him. Growth counseling provides the direction and the stimulation by which the individual is motivated to utilize his current capabilities and develop his capacities for effective, fruitful behavior. With increasing self-confidence gained through continuing successes, the individual will persist in behavior holding the most promising possibilities for satisfying outcomes.

Objectives of growth counseling

Growth counseling has as its main concern the total physiological, sociological, and psychological development and welfare of the individual. His maturation, learning, social and emotional adjustment, and continuous progress are all matters of concern to counseling. It attempts to contribute objectivity and precision to the counseling function within a setting marked by cordiality and acceptance.

The eight items that follow constitute the major objectives of growth counseling, and they serve as performance goals toward which the individual is expected constantly to strive and upon which he is expected continually to improve.

1. Academic and social skills. The individual is to demonstrate academic and social skills and abilities at a level considerably above the typical expectations of the school or the society. The anticipations and expectations of both will not suffice, and mediocrity in performance is unacceptable. The belief is that many youngsters are capable of a higher performance and desirable behavior well above the anticipations of the school. This view assumes a careful consideration by the school of the mental, emotional, and physical capacities of each individual. A keen awareness as to any existing handicaps or deficiencies should exist, and efforts should be made to accommodate the youngster accordingly.

2. A sense of personal responsibility. A demonstrated sense of responsibility for all behaviors, successes, and failures is required. As Glasser (1969) suggests, it is the responsibility of each child to work to succeed and to rise above his environmental handicaps, and it is the responsibility of society to provide a school system in which success is possible.

3. Ability to solve problems. The individual is to demonstrate the ability to solve problems relevant to his education, and occasionally to propose new approaches for solving problems. The idea is one of having an understanding of the concepts within an area and then being able to perform successfully in dealing with the problems.

4. Behavior appropriate to a value system. Behavior should reflect a commitment to a value system and an awareness as to the relevance of that value system to one's own welfare. Conduct is to reflect a commitment to standards prescribed by society and an understanding of the individual's role in society.

5. Behavioral changes and adjustments. Constant changes in behavior appropriate to the continuous accumulation of knowledge and to new skills are expected. Growth denotes developing abilities, the refinement and perfection of skills, and the improvement of motivation. Growth includes both the demonstrated ability and the desire to make needed changes in behavior.

6. Newly developed skills. The individual is expected to demonstrate periodically the acquisition of new skills and productive action toward goal achievement. The refinement of old skills and the attainment of new ones are concomitants of creative endeavors and productive involvements.

7. A developing self-concept. The client is to demonstrate a certain competence in schoolwork and in social activities that denotes a developing self-concept. The individual's behaviors and levels of performance must reflect his current abilities, and they should also reflect the development of new abilities. There must be demonstrable evidence of existing and improving self-confidence and faith in oneself.

8. Appropriate utilization of the environment. The individual is to demonstrate a comprehension of the resources available in the environment and an ability to properly utilize those resources. Research (Longstreth 1968) suggests many implications of this concept for education, as it suggests the need for the most stimulating and enriching environment possible for all learners. The resourceful exploitation of the environment for the benefit of the individual is stressed.

Features of growth counseling

Growth counseling has as its main objective the maximization of the personal growth of each individual. This is done by facilitating each aspect of the person's development and by expediting the learning process. Counseling is designed to bring about a quality relationship in which the person may gain the information, experience the insights, sense the encouragement and reinforcement, and perceive the possibilities open to him. It is from such experiences that the individual begins to sense his own possible greatness, while experiencing the greatest growth possible. The individual is viewed by the counselor as coparticipant in activities designed to promote his maximum growth.

Representative features of growth counseling

The degree to which it is possible to identify every feature or concept of growth counseling is open to question. However, this counseling approach does have some distinguishing features, which are represented in the following pages.

1. Growth through self-initiated action. There is no counseling approach today that may substitute for the will, the initiative, or the self-dependence of the child or the adult. The individual can do more for himself than any counselor or therapist. However, his progress may be enhanced through the aid of a competent counselor and the influence of other responsible adults. Such assistance is more pronounced and ultimately more beneficial if powers of personal persuasion and independence already exist or are in the process of being developed within the child.

2. Growth through continuing internal change. The test of one's effectiveness and ultimate achievement rests with the quality of his internal characteristics. The individual himself determines the nature of his conduct and the heights of his usefulness as a member of a society. The growing, responding child thus experiences a continuous change in his resources, capacities, and attitudes from which behavior changes and adaptations are constantly being made.

The implications for education are many. One suggests that the true worth of an experience is determined by its influence for permanent growth upon the internal capacities of the child. If the child is influenced positively and continues to profit from additional activities triggered by the initial experience, then it has value for him. If no influence for continuing change is felt, the experience is of no value.

The worth of an experience is further determined by what it helps the child to become by virtue of that experience. Positive growth in character and an improvement in personality result from each selected activity. The child's total development is constantly enhanced through growth-promoting experiences.

3. Growth through a continuing influence on others. As the child profits from his interaction with the environment, he can have a positive influence upon other children. There is a reciprocating factor here as he both learns from others and teaches others. The assumption of an attitude of responsibility by the child for the welfare of others results in continuing growth and in consistent effectiveness in his human relationships.

4. Growth through a utilization of the developmental process.

The developmental process includes those systematic changes within the totality of the individual that constitute the esssentials of a human being. These changes are the responses of the organism to the inherent and dynamic powers that prompt and underlie the tendency to unfold, to change, and to grow. The child can both profit from and contribute to this process. He may capitalize upon the natural phenomena of development, and he may also contribute to the quality of that development through self-discipline and the resourceful use of his capabilities.

5. Growth through a full utilization of energies and time. The child's energies are perceived as sources of powerful action from which considerable productivity may result. The human organism is accorded profound respect, and its sources of energies are nurtured and utilized. Time is equated with wealth and is treated accordingly. Each hour must yield an outcome of productive effort. The attitude that time lost is gone forever is constantly stressed.

6. Growth through a use of the self-concept. A positive self-concept remains as an important goal of counseling because of its relevance to learning and to effective functioning. Energies are best utilized by the individual who is at peace with himself and who accepts himself realistically and positively. A positive self-concept is an expected outcome of counseling, and it also serves as a forerunner to an effective counseling relationship.

The techniques of growth counseling

Growth counseling makes no claim to exclusive or unique techniques, nor does it subscribe to a particular approach to the exclusion of all others. It does claim to utilize techniques appropriate to the philosophical and theoretical orientation of the growth-counseling concept. It also recognizes the need to selectively utilize the techniques holding the greatest promise for a particular person with his unique problems. In other words, the concern of growth counseling is essentially one of making certain that the individual continues to grow and to increase in his capabilities and skills and becomes increasingly competent with each new experience.

The flexibility that characterizes this approach permits a utilization of any technique that, according to the best judgment of the counselor, is the best under existing circumstances. For example, some of the behavior modification techniques are sometimes used, although growth counseling is not a strictly behavioristic approach. Advisement and other of the more directive techniques may also be used, but with certain limitations and with the benefit of a deeply caring counselor. The cleverness and competence of the counselor are evident as he involves the client to a high degree in decision making. Even in utilizing advisement, he avoids usurping the prerogatives of the client and continually stresses the personal growth of the individual.

Reflection of feelings. Growth counseling believes in an early expression of and a clarification of existing feelings as a first step toward growth and problem resolution. Reflection also serves a major purpose in creating a warm, stimulating atmosphere in which to work. Such an approach conveys an attitude of genuine caring by the counselor and serves to reduce barriers and minimize any tendency toward client rigidity. The warmth and openness created serve as motivators for client action and reduce anxieties concerning the counseling experience. The techniques of the client-centered approaches are utilized to the degree necessary to effect a fruitful relationship, particularly during the early sessions.

Listening. A concerned, responding listener with a genuine interest in the personal welfare of the individual is viewed as an essential ingredient of all counseling. Listening is thus utilized as an art and as a technique of value in helping a client. It is not a case of just knowing how to remain silent, but rather one of utilizing silence and a listening attitude to the betterment of the therapeutic process.

Reinforcement. The crux of growth counseling is its emphasis upon the internal growth of the individual. It is from this increasing strength that the individual becomes more capable of resolving problems and profiting from his experiences. Growing self-confidence is seen as a most essential ingredient for a successful performance. This self-confidence does not occur automatically, but is, in reality, the result of positive reinforcement and appropriate feedback following the individual's efforts. Reinforcement, through verbal approbation and appropriate rewards, serves as a means toward the goal of high self-confidence.

Establishment of an objective. No matter what the nature of the techniques might be at any one point, there is always a concern for the identification of an objective or goal. This procedure gives structure to the session and encourages intelligent utilization of time and resources. The counselor takes the initiative as needed in helping the client identify goals for a particular session and eventually for the duration of therapy. This is done tactfully and casually as the relationship is developed and as working techniques are proven effective.

Exploration of alternatives. In some approaches, an exploration of alternate courses of action is made for purposes of identifying an early solution to a problem. This is done in group counseling for purposes of stimulating the intellectual capabilities of the individual and helping him see the logic of determining the possible courses of action open to him. This approach also makes it possible to enumerate the merits and limitations of a particular course of action. Choices may then be made on the basis of carefully considered facts, rather than by accident or emotion.

A broadening of experiences. The therapeutic process has its focus during the formal sessions, but it is not limited to these times. The counselor alertly anticipates the needs of his client and unhesitatingly recommends involvement in academic and social activities that hold promise for personal client growth. He also attempts an assessment of a person's skills for purposes of providing some direction toward the improvement and development of needed skills.

The counselor thus extends his sphere of influence to include more than just the counseling session as he encourages and provides some direction for a variety of meaningful experiences.

Relaxation. The relaxation technique permits the counselor to help the individual reach a state of physical and emotional receptivity in which anxiety and any tendency toward resistance are reduced. This technique may be learned rather readily by the counselor, and its utilization in counseling is relatively simple and practical. This approach is always supplemented by a positive attitude toward the welfare of the individual and a demonstrated concern for the total growth process of the individual.

Desensitization. Although desensitization is regarded as more technical and clinically oriented than most other growth-counseling approaches, it is sometimes used. This is closely allied with relaxation, but involves taking the client through specific steps in the desensitization process. The quality of the relationship is really of greater concern than the use of any particular technique. Flexibility characterizes the relationship at all times.

The future of growth counseling

Growth counseling is receptive to the trends and innovations in modern education and to new developments within society. Educational technology is providing for some new and exciting possibilities in counseling. The concept of performance objectives, within a systems approach, is having a tremendous influence upon the techniques being utilized by counselors in their work, and more particularly upon counselor education programs in graduate schools. Aspiring counselors under this type of training program will be expected to achieve prescribed levels in their knowledge, understanding, and counseling skills. A substantial improvement in the competencies of counselors may be expected under this type of program.

Growth counseling not only subscribes to these newer practices in training and application but it is also on the forefront of developing counselor education programs based upon the concept of demonstrated competence as a prerequisite to obtaining a counseling position. The influence of the principles and concepts underlying growth counseling is expected to result in greater counselor effectiveness.

The concepts of personal accountability for one's behavior, the full utilization of one's capacities, experiencing as an essential to one's development, and the intelligent utilization of the environment for personal benefit all have merit for the popularity and usefulness of growth counseling.

Summary

There is a need for a counseling theory that will more adequately meet the needs of individuals seeking assistance with their problems. Growth counseling is an attempt to provide a different philosophical structure from which to operate in order to better accommodate large numbers of clients with a wide variety of problems.

This counseling approach stresses the observance of key commonalities of objectives, principles, and concepts. The concepts and objectives of growth counseling permit a full utilization of the developmental process while simultaneously promoting individual development.

The techniques of growth counseling are inclusive and flexible, permitting the use of approaches regarded by the counselor as most suitable for a particular client. This approach appears to have a promising future in terms of changes and expectations of the society.

Study and discussion problems

1. Describe your reaction to the concept of growth counseling.
   a. Identify its limitations.
   b. Enumerate its possible strengths.
2. Defend the point of view that there is need for a better theoretical framework for the school counselor.
   a. Identify the limitations of current theories.
   b. Point out what is needed to improve theory.
3. List about five advantages that may come from having a theory made up of commonalities.
   a. Note what these commonalities may include.
   b. Add any new ones that you think would be appropriate.
4. Enumerate the main concepts of growth counseling.

    a. Criticize each of these concepts by identifying its strengths and weaknesses.
    b. Add some you think should be included.
5. Make some predictions for the future of counseling theory.
    a. Identify the trends that are likely to influence counseling theory.
    b. Describe counseling of the future.

Appendix

Systems approach in counselor education— performance objectives for each chapter

/ 1 / An introduction to the counseling process

I. Content Classification: This assignment concentrates upon the main themes of this text and upon the meaning of counseling and psychotherapy as essential activities in a modern world.

II. Purposes: The purposes of this assignment include providing you with information and direction that will result in your being well informed and able to demonstrate knowledge and skills on the following topics:

    A. The current view concerning the nature of counseling in a changing world.

    B. The major themes expressed and carried out in this text.

    C. The meaning of counseling and psychotherapy, including formal definitions of these terms.

    D. The significant developments in the field of counseling.

    E. The reasons underlying a need for change in counseling theory.

III. Setting: The setting for accomplishing this assignment will include the classroom and all other suitable study areas, as well as a counseling office or laboratory.

IV. Resources and Activities: The main sources of information and the activities to be engaged in include:
   A. The assigned chapter, discussion problems, and referenced bibliography.
   B. Any available audio-visual aids.
   C. Materials presented by instructor.
   D. Class discussions, oral presentations, and demonstrations.
   E. Role playing.
   F. Actual counseling sessions.

V. Performance Objectives: The objectives for this unit of study suggest that you can, upon the completion of the reading and engaging in appropriate activities, do the following:
   A. Explain the relevance of counseling in today's world.
   B. List the main themes of the text as outlined by the author and make an explanatory statement about each.
   C. Demonstrate a knowledge of counseling and psychotherapy by defining each.
   D. Demonstrate the possession of skills related to the meaning of counseling and of psychotherapy.
   E. Enumerate and explain four or more significant developments in counseling.
   F. Point out five or more implications that these or other developments may have for the practicing counselor or psychotherapist.
   G. Identify five or more conditions in the society that contribute to the need for counseling services.
   H. Outline some major implications that the above have for counselor training programs.
   I. Develop a case for the need for change in counseling theory by identifying three or more limitations of the present theories as you currently understand them.
   J. Enumerate at least one major idea you have gained from

these experiences that will be helpful to you in your own professional development.

  K. Demonstrate an important change in your own behavior as a result of recent experiences associated with this unit.

VI. Evaluation: In addition to, or in conjunction with, the above objectives, the following exercises will be engaged in for purposes of assessing your growth and progress:

  A. Group exercises in which each group member will report on a specified topic and be rated by other group members on a prepared rating sheet.

  B. Role playing exercises and ratings by group members.

  C. Written exercises: essay and completion.

  D. Multiple-choice and/or matching test items.

/ 2 / A theoretical framework for counseling

I. Content Classification: This assignment stresses and permits an understanding of theory as a guide to more effective counseling.

II. Purposes: The purposes of this assignment are to provide you with structured guidelines for study and the necessary activities from which you may become well informed and appropriately skillful in discussing, reporting upon, and demonstrating your competencies on the following representative topics:

  A. The relevance of a theoretical framework to your effectiveness as a counselor.

  B. Why theory is in reality a very practical notion with realistic possibilities for you in counseling.

  C. The true meaning of theory and the role it plays in counseling.

  D. The history and relationship of three major theoretical forces to current theory:

    1. Associationism.

    2. Classical psychoanalysis.

    3. Humanism.

III. Setting: The setting for accomplishing this assignment will include any and all suitable study areas available to you—the classroom, counseling laboratory, and counseling office.

IV. Resources and Activities: The main sources of information and the activities to be utilized include:

    A. The assigned chapter in the text, including the discussion problems.

    B. The bibliography for this chapter found in the appendix.

    C. Special papers or outlines provided by the instructor.

    D. Class lectures and discussions.

    E. Available audio-visual aids:

        1. Tape recordings.

        2. Slide or filmstrip materials.

        3. Films.

    F. Role playing with classmate.

    G. Group discussions.

    H. Oral reports and demonstrations.

    I. Actual counseling sessions.

V. Performance Objectives: You can, upon the completion of the assigned reading, participation in classroom and laboratory experiences, and resourceful experimentation in role playing and counseling, perform the following tasks to the satisfaction of your instructor, your classmates, and yourself:

    A. Draw a graphical representation of a "theoretical framework" and explain it to the class.

    B. Describe and demonstrate how a counselor who works without any theoretical orientation might work.

    C. Describe and demonstrate how a counselor with a theoretical orientation might function in counseling.

    D. Enumerate the main reasons used by some counselors for avoiding the utilization of theory in their counseling.

    E. Defend the point of view that the counselor increases his competence as he properly utilizes theory.

F. Enumerate and explain four or five existing conditions that increase the need for observance of theory in counseling.

G. Outline three or more concepts of associationism that have a close relationship to counseling.

H. Outline three or more concepts of classical psychoanalysis.

I. Enumerate three or four of the main classifications under humanistic psychology:

1. Briefly describe each of these.

2. Name at least one additional theory classification that might be included here.

J. Report on an idea you gained from your reading or experiences that you feel has merit for you and perhaps for other counselors as well.

K. Report or outline a possible notion for a counseling theory that is "way out," or fantastic, and in all probability unacceptable to the conventional counselor.

L. Explain or demonstrate a change in your own thinking and behavior that you feel was prompted by your experiences in this unit.

VI. Evaluation: In order to ascertain the extent of your progress and the degree of your increasing competence, the following evaluation exercises are suggested for use:

A. Ratings by class members on a prepared rating sheet.

B. Ratings by group members or class on a role-playing exercise.

C. Ratings by a role-playing partner or actual client.

D. Written exercises:

1. Essay items.

2. Completion items.

E. Objective questions:

1. Multiple-choice.

2. Matching.

3. True-False.

F. Brief written report covering personal observations and ideas.
G. Observations of instructor and advanced graduate students.

/ 3 / Traditional psychoanalytic theory

I. Content Classification: This assignment deals with the traditional psychoanalytic theory, with emphasis upon its contributions to current theory and to the various counseling and therapeutic approaches.

II. Purposes: The purposes of this unit of study include making possible an increase in your knowledge about this theory, a betterment of your skills, and a fuller refinement of your techniques toward your becoming a more effective counselor and psychotherapist.

III. Setting: The setting for completing this unit of work will include the classroom, available and suitable study areas, counseling offices, and the laboratory.

IV. Resources and Activities: The principal sources of information and the activities to be utilized include:

A. Chapter 3 in the text.
B. The bibliographical references found throughout the chapter.
C. Outlines of this theory as prepared by the class members and the instructor.
D. Class lectures and discussions.
E. Available instructional aids.
F. Group discussions.
G. Group therapy sessions utilizing the technique and observing the theoretical constructs of this theory.
H. Oral reports and demonstrations by class members.
I. Lectures and presentations by available personnel with special expertise with this theory.
J. Role-playing sessions with assigned classmates in individual and group sessions.
K. Actual counseling sessions with clients or patients.

V. Performance Objectives: Given the conditions outlined under III and IV above, you will be able to satisfactorily demonstrate the following performance objectives, or acceptable substitutes as agreed upon with your instructor:

A. Identify the person regarded as the father of psychoanalysis, and:

1. Enumerate five or more relevant facts about him with relevance to this theory.

2. Describe the highlights of his family and personal life.

3. Point out some significant parallels or relationships between his life and experiences and the main elements of his theory.

4. Role-play this individual and answer questions posed by class members concerning "your" work and life.

5. Explain two or three important philosophical points upon which this person based his theory.

B. Name three or four other people who had a close association with the early development of this theory and relate something of interest about each.

C. Enumerate and describe two or three significant developments this theory has experienced.

D. Describe three or more basic assumptions underlying this theory that have had considerable influence upon its history and upon its techniques.

E. Enumerate and explain about five of the main concepts.

F. Identify some important implications that any two of the main concepts may have for the counseling process.

G. Identify about three elements of this theory that have evoked controversy with other theories.

H. Enumerate and describe the principal techniques used.

I. Demonstrate in a role-playing session two or more of the main techniques.

J. Conduct a counseling session in which you clearly apply at least one main concept.

K. Design a graphic representation of this theory in which you stress and clarify at least one of the main assumptions or concepts.

L. Identify at least two important limitations of this theory and explain how these limitations may influence the counselor-client relationship.

M. Explain how you have been influenced by a study of this theory.

VI. Evaluation: In addition to or in conjunction with the performance objectives, you should be prepared to perform on the following to the satisfaction of your instructor or an assigned evaluator:

A. Demonstrate your knowledge of and skill in using this approach in oral or written assignments.

B. Demonstrate your knowledge and understanding by identifying the main concepts, principles, terms, and names associated with this theory through objective examination questions:
1. Matching.
2. Multiple-choice.
3. Open-ended or completion.

C. Demonstrate your ability to explain the highlights of this theory:
1. Essay items.
2. Oral examination.

D. Provide some evidence that denotes a significant change in your behavior as a result of your study and experiences.

E. Outline some proposals showing how you plan to use your new understanding and skills.

/ 4 / Individual psychology

I. Content Classification: This is a unit covering individual psychology, or the Adlerian approach, in counseling and psychotherapy.

II. Purposes: The purposes of this unit are to increase your level of understanding about individual psychology and to help you develop at least minimal skills in its utilization.

III. Setting: The setting for this unit includes the classroom, library, suitable study areas, laboratory, and counseling offices.

IV. Resources and Activities: The principal sources of information and the various possibilities for activities include:

A. The assigned chapter in the text.

B. Appropriate bibliographical references as identified in the chapter.

C. Materials prepared by class members and the instructor.

D. Presentations made in class.

E. Available instructional aids.

F. Discussions within assigned groups dealing with specific topics or problems.

G. Group therapy sessions in which the techniques of this approach are demonstrated.

H. Oral reports, demonstrations, and discussions by class members.

I. Lectures and presentations by individuals within the university or community with a special expertise in this area.

J. Role playing with classmates playing assigned roles as different family members.

K. Counseling sessions with actual family members and complete families.

V. Performance Objectives: Under the conditions outlined above, you will be able to demonstrate the following objectives, or acceptable substitutes, to the satisfaction of your instructor:

A. Identify the person most responsible for individual psychology.

1. Enumerate three or more facts of interest about this individual.

2. Explain the nature of his relationship with Freud.

3. Explain two or three philosophical points upon which this theory was based.

B. Trace the development of this theory by identifying a few other individuals who have followed its teachings.

C. Describe the reaction of counselors to this theory today and point out some significant observations as to its use.

D. Enumerate in your own words one or two basic assumptions or underlying philosophies that seem to characterize this theory.

E. Enumerate and explain about five of the main elements of this theory.

F. Point out the elements that you feel are most logical and acceptable in counseling today and defend your choices.

G. Compare the highlights of this theory with the main elements of the traditional psychoanalytic theory and select those you feel are most correct.

H. Enumerate the main techniques observed and the instruments most likely to be used.

I. Engage in a role-playing session in which you act as the counselor and demonstrate the main techniques of this approach.

J. Conduct a counseling session in which you clearly apply two or more of the concepts of this approach.

K. Draw a graphic representation, or conduct a demonstration with a family, in which you clearly show the use this approach has.

L. Criticize three or more of the elements and explain to the class the possible limitations inherent in this approach.

M. Explain how you have been influenced in your thinking by your study and experiences.

N. Outline or explain your predictions as to the continuing successful use of this approach.

VI. Evaluation: The evaluation techniques used will closely parallel the performance objectives and will permit you to more fully demonstrate your knowledge of this approach and your skills in using it to the satisfaction of your instructors and assigned observers.

A. Demonstrate your understanding of this approach by making verbal or written explanations as requested.

B. Demonstrate your knowledge and understanding of this theory, identifying its main elements, principles, and aims through objective examination questions:
   1. Matching.
   2. Multiple-choice.
   3. True-False.

C. Demonstrate your knowledge of this theory through written and oral expression:
   1. Essay terms.
   2. Oral exercises.
   3. Open-ended statements.

D. Demonstrate your ability to utilize this theory in counseling sessions in which you will be rated by assigned evaluators.

E. Explain, either orally or in writing, the new insights you have gained from your experiences and point out the implications each has for you as a counselor.

/ 5 / Client-centered counseling

I. Content Classification: This unit deals with the client-centered approach in counseling and psychotherapy.

II. Purposes: The purposes of this unit include your becoming sufficiently well acquainted with the key concepts of this theory to explain them to others and sufficiently skillful to demonstrate the techniques to the satisfaction of the class and your instructor.

III. Setting: The setting for the needed activities includes the available study, practice, and performance areas, such as the library, laboratories, classroom, and counseling offices.

IV. Resources and Activities: All meaningful sources of information will be utilized, and a variety of activities will be engaged in for purposes of helping you become proficient in the use of this approach. You are encouraged to be resourceful and imaginative in locating additional sources of information and in practicing your developing skills. The basic sources and activities will include:

A. The assigned reading as provided in the course syllabus.
B. The additional references as identified in the reading.
C. Outlines and materials provided by the instructor and other class members.
D. Presentations and demonstrations presented in class and laboratory sessions.
E. Instructional aids such as video tapes, audio tapes, overhead transparencies, films, and posters.
F. Group discussions in which group members will assume responsibility for certain topics and will evaluate the presentations of other group members.
G. Group sessions used to provide experiences in leading a group and in working as a group member, in dealing with personal development and adjustment problems.
H. Oral reports, demonstrations, and group discussions.
I. Lectures, presentations, or demonstrations by the instructor and by invited experts.
J. Role playing with classmate or assigned coached client.
K. Actual counseling sessions with clients seeking assistance.

V. Performance Objectives: During or upon the completion of the suggested activities, you will be able to carry out the following performances to the satisfaction of your instructors and classmates:
A. Identify the person most responsible for this approach.
1. Enumerate three or more facts of interest about him.
2. Identify and explain some philosophical concepts that characterize his thinking.
3. Explain his major objections to the more conventional approaches.
B. Trace the historical development of this theory.

1. Name other people who have had a close association with it.
2. Describe the nature of the controversies that have surrounded it.
3. Point out its major differences from other approaches.

C. Enumerate and explain the main themes or basic assumptions of this theory.
   1. Relate these themes to philosophy.
   2. Relate these themes to practice.

D. Identify the philosophical points you feel are most consistent with your own philosophy and explain how you are using these elements in your efforts to improve your skills.

E. Enumerate the core concepts of this theory and show how these relate to the anticipated developments in counseling.

F. Describe the principal counseling or therapeutic techniques used.

G. Identify some other theories that you feel have drawn ideas and techniques from the client-centered approach, and briefly describe these ideas.

H. Enumerate at least eight of the twelve main concepts given in Chapter 5 and explain their meaning.

I. Demonstrate in a role-playing situation four or more of the concepts of this approach.

J. Conduct an actual counseling session in which you clearly demonstrate three or more of the concepts.

K. Draw a graph or make an outline with which you can clearly explain this theory to another person.

L. Criticize six or more of the concepts and include what you regard as some critical limitations of the approach.

M. Explain how your own thinking has been influenced by your experiences.

N. Demonstrate some actual changes in your behavior as a result of your study.

VI. Evaluation: An evaluation of your performance, skills, and knowledge will be taking place at all times. The specifics of evaluation will be followed, however, with the expectation that your performances will meet the criteria established for the class and that they will be to the satisfaction of your instructors and assigned observers.

A. Demonstrate your understanding of this theory by responding to requests made, in either verbal or written form.

B. Demonstrate your knowledge of this theory by identifying its main elements, principles, and the people associated with it through objective questions.
   1. Matching.
   2. Multiple-choice.
   3. True-False.

C. Demonstrate your familiarity with this theory through written and oral expressions.
   1. Essay items.
   2. Open-ended items.
   3. Oral reports.

D. Demonstrate your skills to utilize this approach in counseling sessions; you will be evaluated on prepared checklists by assigned observers.

E. Enumerate and explain orally or in writing the insights you feel you have gained from your study.

F. Explain the implications this theory has for you as a counselor and make a prediction as to your possible success as a counselor.

/ 6 / Learning theory approaches applied to counseling

I. Content Classification: This unit deals with the main learning theory approaches related to counseling theory.

II. Purposes: The purposes include your becoming sufficiently well informed about the learning theory approaches to explain the highlights of each theory and sufficiently skillful to demonstrate each.

III. Setting: The center of activity will be the college classroom, but the library, other study areas, laboratories, counseling offices, and observation areas such as classrooms of children will also be included.

IV. Resources and Activities: All appropriate and meaningful sources of available information will be utilized. You are expected to seek additional sources and to experiment with some innovative activities during this unit of study.

A. The assigned chapter and references as included in the course syllabus.

B. Additional references as identified in the reading.

C. Materials prepared and shared by the instructor and class members.

D. Class discussions, demonstrations, and materials utilized in the laboratories.

E. Instructional aids including video tapes, audio tapes, overhead transparencies, films, and bulletin board displays.

F. Group sessions in which a member leads the discussion on a particular topic.

G. Participation in a group therapy session in which you will serve as group leader, and in other sessions in which you will be a group member.

H. Participation as a client in a session in which you are taken through the counseling experience by an advanced graduate student.

I. Participation as a member of a panel that will present some aspect of the theory to the class.

J. Lectures, presentations, and demonstrations by an invited expert.

K. Role-playing sessions with classmates or assigned coached client.

L. Actual counseling sessions with bona fide clients.

V. Performance Objectives: During or upon the completion of the assigned activities, or suitable substitutions, you will be able to meet the following performance objectives to the satisfaction of your instructor or assigned evaluators:

   A. Provide two or three facts related to the background of learning theory, including:
      1. Historically significant information.
      2. Its relationship to educational practice.

   B. Outline the highlights of reinforcement theory.
      1. Name the individuals most closely associated with it.
      2. Enumerate the main elements or concepts.

   C. Outline the highlights of classical conditioning.
      1. Identify some people associated with this approach.
      2. Enumerate the principal elements.

   D. Explain the meaning and use of reciprocal inhibition.
      1. Identify its main philosophical points.
      2. Give its explanations for problem behavior.

   E. Explain the meaning of operant conditioning.
      1. Relate the term to current counseling approaches.
      2. Interpret the explanation it uses to account for behavior.

   F. Outline the highlights of behavioral counseling.
      1. Name individuals having a close association with it.
      2. Identify and explain the main concepts.

   G. Explain the main techniques of each approach, choosing any three of the following:
      1. Reinforcement.
      2. Classical conditioning.
      3. Reciprocal inhibition.
      4. Operant conditioning.
      5. Behaviorism.

   H. Demonstrate in role-playing any two of the above.

   I. Conduct an actual counseling session using the main techniques of any of the theories listed under G above.

J. Critique any two of the theories listed under G above.

    1. Identify the main elements.

    2. Point out the principal limitations of these elements.

K. Explain the main contributions the learning theories have made to other leading approaches.

L. Identify and enumerate some significant changes in your thinking as a result of your study.

M. Explain, and if possible demonstrate, some changes in your counseling techniques as outcomes of the influences of learning theories.

VI. Evaluation: Informal evaluation will take place with your activities under the topic headed "performance objectives." More specific evaluation procedures will be followed, and established criteria will be met to the satisfaction of your instructors.

A. Demonstrate your understanding by engaging in discussions and answering questions posed by class members and the instructors.

B. Demonstrate a fairly comprehensive knowledge by identifying, in objective tests, the main concepts of each division under learning theory:

    1. Reinforcement.

    2. Classical conditioning.

    3. Reciprocal inhibition.

    4. Operant conditioning.

    5. Behaviorism.

C. Demonstrate a familiarity with each of the above areas through written and/or oral examinations.

D. Demonstrate your skills in utilizing any two of the above in counseling sessions; you will be evaluated by assigned observers on a prepared evaluation form.

E. Enumerate the major implications the learning theory approaches have for you as a counselor, in written or oral form as requested.

/ 7 / The trait-factor approach

I. Content Classification: This unit focuses upon the trait-factor approach in counseling. It has a long history and is often associated with the early work of Frank Parsons. It has also been a source of controversy with the client-centered approach.

II. Purposes: The purposes of this unit include helping you become knowledgeable about this approach and skillful in its use.
   A. To know the relevant facts.
   B. To be well acquainted with background information.
   C. To know the place of this approach in current counseling.

III. Setting: The focus of activities will be the university classroom, but other facilities will be utilized:
   A. Library.
   B. University counseling center.
   C. Public school counseling offices.
   D. Laboratory.
   E. Observation areas.
   F. Counseling offices.

IV. Resources and Activities: A variety of resources for reading and activities will be available for this unit. Innovation and initiative on your part in utilizing unspecified sources and in engaging in meaningful experiences are expected.
   A. The assigned chapter and references identified in the chapter or class syllabus.
   B. Outlines and materials prepared by the instructor or class members.
   C. Any available instructional aids.
   D. Papers or special documents.
   E. Participation as a panel member in presenting information.
   F. Participation in a group in which you lead the discussion on an assigned topic.
   G. Role-playing assignment in which you gain experience as a client and as a counselor.

V. Performance Objectives: It is assumed that you will be able to explain the main philosophical positions of this approach and be able to demonstrate the essential techniques used. You will also be able to perform to the satisfaction of your instructors on several specific objectives or suitable substitutions.

   A. Enumerate the important historical facts.
      1. Name the individuals associated with this approach and give two or three important facts about each.
      2. Identify two or three important conditions within society that relate to this approach.
      3. Describe the status of this theory today.
      4. Identify three or four main points of controversy.
   B. Outline or diagram this approach and explain its main elements to the class.
   C. Enumerate and explain the main techniques used and show how each technique relates to the philosophy that underlies the theory.
   D. Demonstrate the main techniques in a role playing or actual counseling session.
   E. Criticize the main concepts of this approach.
      1. Enumerate at least three main concepts and point out the possible weaknesses or limitations.
      2. Identify three or more concepts and defend their merits.
   F. Explain how your study of this approach has helped you personally.
   G. Demonstrate some changes in your counseling techniques that you may attribute to your study in this unit.

VI. Evaluation: Evaluation is an ongoing process throughout the total course; you will be expected to perform satisfactorily in accordance with the criteria used. More formal techniques and instruments will be used, however, for purposes of helping you and your instructors assess your progress. You will be expected to do any of the following, or acceptable substitutes:

A. Respond to questions posed by assigned evaluators in an oral examination.
B. Demonstrate your understanding of this approach by identifying its main elements or concepts and the names of individuals by responding to items on objective questions:
    1. Matching.
    2. Multiple-choice.
    3. True-False.
C. Demonstrate your knowledge and understanding through essay or open-ended items.
D. Demonstrate your skills in utilizing this approach in role-playing sessions with assigned clients, or in real counseling sessions, as determined by assigned observers utilizing a prepared checklist or specified criteria.
E. Enumerate and explain verbally or in writing the insights you have gained from your study.
F. Identify three or more implications this approach has for the counselor.
G. Predict your own chances for success with this approach.
H. Identify and explain any philosophical point emphasized by this approach that is influencing you toward some needed behavior changes.

/ 8 / Developmental counseling

 I. Content Classification: This is a unit on developmental counseling. This approach incorporates several philosophical viewpoints and stresses the notion that the developmental process should be utilized in the counseling relationship.
 II. Purposes: The purposes of this unit include your becoming sufficiently well informed to explain the main concepts of this approach and to counsel effectively utilizing these concepts.
III. Setting: Although the center of activity will be the classroom, you are expected to utilize any available suitable study and practice area:

A. Laboratories.

B. Counseling offices.

C. Library.

IV. Resources and Activities: It is assumed that you will be imaginative, resourceful, and creative in capitalizing upon all possible resources and in engaging in a variety of activities.

    A. The assigned chapter in the text and the discussion problems.

    B. The appropriate bibliographical references for this unit.

    C. The syllabus, outlines, and other materials provided by the instructor.

    D. Class discussions, lectures, and student presentations.

    E. Available instructional aids.

    F. Field trips to observe children in action.

    G. Group and panel presentations.

    H. Lectures and demonstrations by local specialists.

    I. Role-playing experiences and demonstrations.

    J. Actual counseling sessions with groups and with individuals, including children.

V. Performance Objectives: After having made an intensive study of the material and engaged in a variety of activities, you will be able to demonstrate your knowledge of this approach and your competence in counseling to the satisfaction of your instructors. Acceptable substitutes for any of the following objectives may be considered.

    A. Name the individuals most closely associated with the history and development of this approach.

      1. Enumerate some relevant facts about each.

      2. Identify some philosophical concepts underlying the thinking of these individuals.

      3. Point out the major objections these individuals have to any other one theory with which they are in disagreement.

    B. Show how this approach relates to or differs from the traditional psychoanalytic approach or the Adlerian approach.

    C. Outline the main themes or basic assumptions of this theory.

D. Enumerate the main concepts of this approach and relate each to a counseling technique.

E. Identify and explain the main techniques used in counseling.
   1. Explain why these are used in terms of the theory's goals.
   2. Describe additional techniques you feel should be considered.

F. Name a theory closely allied with the developmental approach and explain the relationship; do the same with a theory that is quite different.

G. Demonstrate this approach in a role-playing situation, making certain that the philosophy underlying this approach is made clear to your observers.

H. Criticize at least four of the main concepts.
   1. Identify the apparent strengths.
   2. Identify the limitations.
   3. Suggest some needed changes in the theory.

I. Explain how your thinking has been influenced by your study and experiences.

J. Demonstrate a change in your behavior, personally or as a counselor, as a result of your work in this unit.

K. Identify some important implications that this approach has for counseling and psychotherapy.

VI. Evaluation: In addition to your involvement in the performance objectives and the evaluation provided at the time of the activity, you will work through some exercises designed to assess your progress and level of achievements. Established criteria, instructor's judgments, and prepared instruments will be used.

A. Demonstrate your understanding of this theory in oral and written form, in response to questions posed by instructors and class members.

B. Demonstrate your knowledge by identifying the main elements, principles, and concepts of this theory through objective tests:
   1. Matching.

2. Multiple-choice.

3. True-False.

4. Completion.

C. Demonstrate your skill in utilizing the techniques of this approach in role playing with coached clients, or in real counseling sessions, as evaluated by observers on prepared checklists or evaluation sheets.

D. Identify some important insights you have gained and explain how you may now improve.

E. Identify and explain the principal implications this theory has for you as a counselor.

/ 9 / Rational-emotive therapy

I. Content Classification: This unit deals with rational-emotive psychotherapy, a relatively new approach developed by Dr. Albert Ellis. This approach stresses the importance of thinking logically and realistically about oneself.

II. Purposes: The purposes of this unit include your becoming well acquainted with this approach and able to demonstrate its techniques.

A. The main philosophical viewpoints.

B. The principal concepts.

C. The best techniques.

III. Setting: Since this approach lends itself to approaches somewhat different from those of other theories, you will be expected to go beyond the classroom for many of your experiences. A base of operation is still necessary, however, and this will be the classroom. Other centers of activity will include a variety of places:

A. Counseling laboratories or offices.

B. Library facilities.

C. Study or counseling room in your home.

D. Community clinics or hospitals.

IV. Resources and Activities: You should take considerable initiative in locating suitable reading material and in engaging in a variety of activities from which you can learn and improve your skills.

A. Books written by Albert Ellis.

B. Journal articles by Ellis and articles written by others about this theory.

C. The bibliography included in the syllabus.

D. Special papers and outlines provided by the instructor and class members.

E. Instructional aids:
   1. Video tapes.
   2. Audio tapes.
   3. Films of Ellis using this approach.

F. Observations in which you see a skilled technician using this approach.

G. Lectures and demonstrations by qualified local individuals.

H. Panel discussions and presentations.

I. Class discussions and presentations by class members.

J. Role-playing experiences and demonstrations.

K. Serve as a member of or conduct a group therapy session.

L. Conduct actual counseling sessions with clients.

V. Performance Objectives: In addition to your being able to demonstrate a knowledge and comprehension of this theory, you will develop and demonstrate the appropriate techniques. Suitable substitutes or modifications in these objectives are acceptable, and in some cases encouraged. The level or quality of performance should meet the criteria established and satisfy your instructors.

A. Identify the individual primarily responsible for this theory.
   1. Cite some facts about him.
   2. Describe this individual by noting relevant personality characteristics.
   3. Note his major objections to the psychoanalytic theory.

B. Enumerate and explain the main philosophical points underlying this theory.

C. Diagram or outline this theory and explain its main premises.

D. Identify the main concepts of this theory, by referring to the text if necessary, and explain at least two of the following in your own words:
   1. What the concept means to you.
   2. The implications the concept has for human behavior.
   3. The implications the concept has for you as a counselor.
E. Explain the main techniques used in this approach.
   1. Relate each technique to a goal of therapy.
   2. Add an additional technique you feel would be acceptable in this theory.
F. Identify two other theories with similar concepts or elements and explain why you selected them.
G. Make a brief presentation to the class in which you either defend or attack this theory.
H. Criticize either verbally or in writing two or more of the main concepts.
   1. Identify the most promising strengths.
   2. Identify and explain the limitations.
   3. Point out how the theory might be improved through changes in the concepts.
I. Make a diagram or outline in which you identify some beliefs that have characterized your thinking. Now show what your current thinking is on these particular points after your study in this unit.
J. In addition to making an explanation about how you feel your behavior has changed as a result of your learning, actually role-play or otherwise demonstrate this. You must convince your audience.
K. Identify and explain the most important implications this theory has for counseling and psychotherapy. Do the same for:
   1. The family.
   2. Education or the instructional process.
   3. Society.

VI. Evaluation: In addition to the performance objectives, upon which you will be evaluated, more formal kinds of evaluation procedures will also be used. These will involve the use of established criteria, checklists, open-ended statements, and other available instruments. An expected standard of performance and the assessment of your instructors will be utilized.

    A. Demonstrate your understanding of this theory through written or oral responses to your instructors.

    B. Demonstrate your knowledge of the philosophy, history, principles, concepts, and techniques of this theory through responses to objective examination questions:

        1. Matching.

        2. Multiple choice.

        3. True-False.

        4. Completion.

    C. Demonstrate your ability to utilize the techniques of this theory.

    D. Explain at least one major idea you have gained that will be helpful in making some personal improvements.

    E. Explain or demonstrate changes in your current behavior, attributable to your study of this theory.

/ 10 /   Reality therapy

I. Content Classification: Reality therapy constitutes a relatively new approach in counseling and psychotherapy and is the focus of attention in this unit. It also has application possibilities in the classroom and in the family.

II. Purposes: It is the purpose of this unit to help you become sufficiently well informed to demonstrate satisfactorily your knowledge and skills.

    A. Relate the important facts and information.

    B. Identify the limitations and strengths of the various concepts.

    C. Demonstrate the skills needed to counsel with this approach.

III. Setting: It is the intent to have you explore a number of settings and resources as important parts of your work in this unit. The classroom will serve as the center for an exchange of ideas and information, but you will also explore the following:

    A. Library.

    B. Counseling offices in available elementary and secondary schools.

    C. University counseling center.

    D. Observation offices.

    E. Laboratory.

    F. Counseling offices.

IV. Resources and Activities: All suitable resources should be utilized, and a variety of activities should be engaged in.

    A. Assigned reading in the syllabus.

    B. Outlines and papers.

    C. Available instructional aids.

    D. Lectures and classroom presentations.

    E. Panel preparations and presentations.

    F. Participation as a leader or member of a therapy group.

    G. Demonstrations and presentations by class members and by available individuals with special expertise.

V. Performance Objectives: By observing the conditions described above, you will be able to demonstrate the following objectives, or appropriate substitutes, in accordance with the criteria provided and to the satisfaction of the instructor.

    A. Name and describe the person responsible for this approach.

        1. Enumerate a few facts of interest about him.

        2. Describe the kinds of activities and experiences he has been engaged in.

        3. Enumerate two or more philosophical points of view that reflect his thinking.

    B. Trace the highlights of this theory's development.

    C. Describe your initial feelings about this theory as you begin a more intensive study of it.

    D. Enumerate four or more of the most important or central concepts.

        1. Show how these relate to personality development.

        2. Show how they relate to counseling.

    E. Identify the main differences this theory has from the traditional psychoanalytic theory.

    F. Describe the principal techniques used.

    G. Conduct a role-playing session in which you demonstrate the main techniques.

    H. Criticize about four of the concepts.

        1. Identify the most obvious limitations.

        2. Identify and defend what you regard as the main strengths.

    I. Describe at least one major idea you have gained from your study.

        1. Explain how you plan to capitalize upon this idea.

        2. Propose an original idea you feel has merit.

    J. Make a prediction as to the possible future of this theory, taking into consideration conditions and trends in the society.

VI. Evaluation: Some parallels between the performance objectives and the evaluation techniques are both desirable and inevitable. This section, however, provides you with a greater opportunity to demonstrate more precisely your skills with this approach.

    A. Demonstrate your knowledge by responding verbally to questions posed by class members and by the instructor.

    B. Prove your ability to identify the main concepts, principles, and techniques by responding to objective questions and problems.

        1. Matching.

        2. Multiple-choice.

        3. True-False.

        4. Fill in the blanks.

    C. Demonstrate your ability to use the techniques in counseling sessions with coached or legitimate clients.

1. Ratings will be given by assigned observers on a prepared rating sheet.
2. Observations will be made by instructors and supervisors.
D. Explain either orally or in writing at least one main insight you have gained from your study.
E. Demonstrate in a role-playing situation in a personal, but noncounseling session, changes in your behavior that have occurred by virtue of your study.

/ 11 / Gestalt therapy

I. Content Classification: This unit deals directly with a therapeutic approach called gestalt therapy. It has a close relationship with the learning theories, and also follows many of the reality therapy concepts. Its use in an educational setting is somewhat limited, having better possibilities in a clinical setting.
II. Purposes: The purposes of this unit are quite broad, including your becoming sufficiently well informed with this theory to explain satisfactorily the main elements and to demonstrate its principal techniques.
A. Relate the important facts.
B. Identify the main elements and criticize each.
C. Demonstrate your skill as a counselor.
III. Setting: The center of formal activity will be the classroom, but with considerable opportunity to extend your activities to a variety of settings:
A. Library.
B. Available counseling offices in nearby public schools.
C. Counseling offices in the university.
D. Counseling laboratory.
E. Home and neighborhood.
F. Various social settings.
IV. Resources and Activities. All available resources of materials and data will be used, and a variety of activities will be made available for broad and intensive involvement:

A. Assigned reading in the syllabus.
B. Books and journal articles.
C. Classroom lectures.
D. Special papers and outlines.
E. Participation in classroom discussions.
F. Oral presentations and demonstrations for other class members.
G. Role playing with a coached client.

V. Performance Objectives: If you make an intensive study of this theory and engage in a number of activities, you will be able to satisfactorily perform the following objectives, or acceptable substitutes.

A. Name the individuals historically responsible for the development of this theory.
1. Enumerate information of interest.
2. Describe the nature of their activities.

B. Trace the historical highlights of this theory, including:
1. Its relationship to other theories.
2. Its controversial elements.

C. Describe your first reactions to the theory, including:
1. What you like.
2. The elements or philosophies you question.

D. Enumerate the main philosophical views or assumptions underlying this approach.

E. Enumerate all six of the main concepts as given in the chapter.
1. Explain each in your own words.
2. Relate each to at least one other theory.

F. Identify any unique or interesting elements.
1. Explain what makes them unique or interesting.
2. Use your own imagination and explain how you think these elements could be improved upon.

G. Describe the techniques that are most frequently and successfully used.

H. Describe a group setting in which this approach is used.

I. Function as a group leader in a therapy group made up of class members.

J. Conduct a counseling session with a coached or legitimate client using this approach.

K. Criticize two or more of the main concepts.

   1. Defend the position of gestalt therapist.

   2. Identify the principal limitations.

VI. Evaluation: After having engaged in a variety of experiences leading up to and including the performance objectives, you will be ready for some more intensive and formal evaluation activities. Certain criteria, evaluation instruments, and procedures will be provided by your instructors. They will also determine an acceptable level of performance in each case.

A. Demonstrate your understanding by engaging in evaluative discussions based upon specific questions and problems dealing with this approach.

B. Demonstrate a reasonable level of knowledge of this theory through the use of objective questions.

   1. Matching.

   2. Multiple-choice.

C. Demonstrate your ability to use this approach with a coached client.

D. Explain in writing at least one major idea you gained from your study.

   1. Account for the occurrence of this idea.

   2. Explain how you plan to use this idea.

E. Demonstrate some significant changes in your own behavior.

   1. Show how these changes relate to some theoretical element of gestalt therapy.

   2. Perform an act that will illustrate your new thoughts.

/ 12 / Logotherapy

I. Content Classification: This unit deals with logotherapy as a counseling and psychotherapeutic approach. Its philosophical viewpoints have utilization value in many aspects of human relationships and in education. An understanding of logotherapy provides a foundation for a deeper appreciation for mankind and for man's many problems.

II. Purposes: The central purpose of this unit is for you to develop a feeling and an appreciation for logotherapy and to increase your counseling skills.

A. To identify the main philosophical points.

B. To describe how these philosophies may be applied in counseling.

III. Setting: To gain an appropriate feeling for this philosophy, it will be necessary to explore and to experiment rather widely. However, the exchange of ideas and the reporting of findings will take place primarily in the classroom and laboratories.

IV. Resources and Activities: A variety of reading sources will be utilized, and activities designed to sharpen your awareness of logotherapy, and to better your counseling skills, will be provided.

A. Syllabus and outlines.

B. Papers and documents.

C. Lectures, demonstrations, discussions, and presentations.

V. Performance Objectives: Obviously, some kinds of experiences will be more meaningful to you than others. Your involvement in a study of this unit should be a source of excitement and satisfaction to you. Flexibility in activities will thus characterize your work. The following performance objectives will serve as guidelines in the determination of the skills you should be able to demonstrate. These objectives, or substitutes acceptable to you and your instructors, will be within your capabilities throughout your study of this unit.

A. Relate some significant facts about logotherapy, including:

   1. Its founder and highlights of his life.
   2. A brief history of its development.
B. Describe your reactions to this philosophy.
   1. Account for your feelings in terms of your own beliefs.
   2. Point out how you think this philosophy can best be used.
C. Outline its main philosophical points or basic assumptions.
   1. Explain this to a group who know little or nothing about logotherapy.
   2. Illustrate each point, emphasizing simplicity and logic.
D. Enumerate and explain the six main concepts.
   1. Diagram or give illustrations of two or more.
   2. Add at least one concept you think would be appropriate.
E. Report two or three of the main techniques used.
   1. Explain each.
   2. Demonstrate each.
F. Conduct a counseling session in which you clearly demonstrate this approach, including:
   1. The philosophy underlying it.
   2. The therapeutic elements.
G. Describe how this approach might be used with a group, including:
   1. The most promising techniques.
   2. The anticipated outcomes.
H. Criticize three or more of the main concepts.
   1. Identify some important strengths.
   2. Deliberately question two of the philosophical viewpoints.
VI. Evaluation: Many of the ideas included are essentially philosophical, and thus difficult to objectify. However, it is essential that you have a basic understanding of this philosophy and a genuine feeling for it. Each evaluation exercise is designed to help you achieve the goals you have had in mind for yourself in this unit. You will help determine the level of performance you expect of yourself in cooperation with your instructors.
A. Demonstrate your knowledge by briefly highlighting this phi-

losophy before a group of your classmates who will evaluate your presentation.

B. Demonstrate your ability to utilize the concepts through a counseling session with a coached client.

C. Demonstrate your knowledge by listing and explaining the main points.

D. Explain in writing at least one insight you gained from your study.

E. Convince the class of some significant behavior change you have made.

F. Enumerate two or three implications this philosophy has for counseling.

/ 13 / Existentialism in counseling and psychotherapy

I. Content Classification: This unit deals with existentialism, a philosophy that underlies several of the current counseling approaches. We have an interest in it because of the possibilities it holds for contributions to counseling and psychotherapy. We look to it for ideas concerning the nature of man and for other philosophical concepts that might be integrated with selected counseling techniques.

II. Purposes: The purposes include your becoming sufficiently well acquainted with existentialism to enumerate its principal ideas and to point out several important implications that it has for the counseling profession.

III. Setting: The principal area of activity will be the classroom, but other areas will be utilized:

A. Library.

B. Laboratories.

C. Observation areas.

D. Clinics, hospitals, and rest homes where available.

IV. Resources and Activities: Wide reading combined with meaningful discussions are critical to your becoming acquainted with this philosophy. You are encouraged to explore widely and to take advantage of all useful resources available to you.

  A. Class syllabus and outlines.

  B. Class lectures and demonstrations.

  C. Instructional aids.

  D. Group discussions.

  E. Participation as a panel member in presenting information on assigned topics.

V. Performance Objectives: Since many elements of existentialism are philosophical and even nebulous, to perform a particular objective may be more difficult than is the case with some clear-cut counseling approach. However, it will be possible for you to demonstrate a knowledge of and a feeling for the philosophy during and upon the completion of this unit.

  A. Outline the historical background of existentialism.

  B. Relate the relationship between selected elements of this philosophy and education itself.

  C. Enumerate three or more implications it has for the counseling profession.

  D. Identify three or four acceptable counseling techniques that you feel best fit existentialism.

  E. Criticize the main elements of this philosophy in terms of your own beliefs.

    1. Present the ideas most acceptable to you.

    2. Present a case against any unacceptable ideas.

IV. Evaluation: Hopefully, you will be able to satisfy yourself concerning your knowledge and understanding as you move through this unit. To help you objectify your level of knowledge and your counseling skills, certain evaluation exercises will be utilized. Deletions or substitutions are always possible in these evaluation experiences.

  A. Demonstrate your understanding by responding to questions posed by class members and the instructor.

B. Demonstrate your knowledge by responding to prepared objective questions.

C. Demonstrate your counseling skill by using techniques appropriate to this philosophy in a role-playing situation with a class member or assigned client.

D. Prove your understanding by listing some important implications this philosophy has for all counseling.

E. Identify at least one major concept from existentialism that has had a significant impact upon your thinking.

1. Write this with the necessary detail.

2. Explain the nature of its influence upon you.

/ 14 / Growth counseling as a contributor to counseling theory

I. Content Classification: This unit deals with growth counseling, as a concept against which the major counseling theories were criticized in this publication. This unit provides opportunities for learning about the need for theory in counseling and for learning more about the nature of growth counseling. It also provides some direction for the development of new ideas that may have merit for making current theories more meaningful.

II. Purposes: The purposes of this unit include helping you become sufficiently well informed to explain the meaning of growth counseling and to enumerate its main concepts. You should also become sufficiently motivated from your study that ideas for the improvement of counseling should occur to you. Your counseling skills should also be improved upon as you translate your ideas into practice.

III. Setting: Most of your formal study will be centered in the usual places, including the library, classroom, and laboratories. It is also recommended that you utilize other areas that may provide meaningful learning experiences.

IV. Resources and Activities: The text chapter constitutes the main source of reading, but appropriate references will also be utilized.

A fairly comprehensive understanding of all the theories is an essential prerequisite to a meaningful study of this chapter.

A. Class syllabus, outlines, and papers.

B. Lectures, demonstrations, and class discussions.

C. Instructional aids:

    1. Tapes.

    2. Transparencies.

    3. Slides.

V. Performance Objectives: The main performances in this unit are based upon an understanding of growth counseling and upon your ability to demonstrate both your understanding and your counseling skills. Upon the completion of this unit, you should be able to perform to the satisfaction of your instructors a number of skills. Appropriate substitutions may be made as seems advisable to the instructor.

A. Make a brief outline highlighting the need for a better theory.

B. Enumerate the three counseling commonalities covered in the chapter and show how each relates to effective counseling.

C. Criticize orally any six of the twelve principles covered in the chapter.

D. Explain in your own words the main philosophical views underlying growth counseling.

E. Enumerate and explain some important objectives for any kind of counseling.

    1. Show how your list differs from or resembles the objectives discussed in the chapter.

    2. Point out some weaknesses in the objectives given in the text.

F. Relate each of the six major features of growth counseling to your own notions about what counseling should be.

G. Demonstrate your counseling skill in a real or role-playing situation observing the guidelines of this approach.

H. Explain in writing how your thinking has been influenced by your present study.

Bibliography

Arbuckle, D. S. 1965. *Counseling: Philosophy, theory and practice.* Boston: Allyn and Bacon.

Arnold, M. 1960. *Emotion and personality.* New York: Columbia University Press.

Aubrey, R. F. 1967. The effect of counselors on the reward system of teachers. *The Personnel and Guidance Journal* 45 (10):1017–1020.

Beck, C. E. 1963. *Philosophical foundations of guidance.* Englewood Cliffs, N. J.: Prentice-Hall.

Berenson, B. G., and Carkhuff, R. R. 1967. *Sources of gain in counseling and psychotherapy.* New York: Holt, Rinehart and Winston.

Blocher, D. H. 1966. *Developmental counseling.* New York: Ronald Press.

Blocher, D. H. 1968. Developmental counseling: A rationale for counseling in the elementary school. *Elementary School Guidance and Counseling* 2 (3):163–172.

Bower, E. M., and Hollister, W. G. 1967. *Behavioral science frontiers in education.* New York: Wiley.

Bruce, Paul. 1966. Three forces in psychology and their ethical and educational implications. *The Educational Forum* 30 (3):277–285.

Carkhuff, R. R., and Berenson, B. G. 1967. *Beyond counseling and therapy.* New York: Holt, Rinehart and Winston.

Chenault, J. 1968. Counseling theory: the problem of definition. *Personnel and Guidance Journal* 47 (2):110–114.

Christensen, O. C. 1969. Education: A model for counseling in the elementary school. *Elementary School Guidance and Counseling* 4 (1):12–19.

Corsini, R., ed. 1973. *Current psychotherapies.* Itasca, Illinois: F. E. Peacock.

Dimick, K. M., and Huff, V. E. 1970. *Child counseling.* Dubuque, Iowa: Wm. C. Brown.

Dinkmeyer, D. C. 1965. *Child development: The emerging self.* Englewood Cliffs, N.J.: Prentice-Hall.

Dinkmeyer, D. C. 1966. Developmental counseling in the elementary school. *Personnel and Guidance Journal* 45 (3):262–266.

Dinkmeyer D. C. 1967. Counseling theory and practice in the elementary school. *Elementary School Guidance and Counseling* 1 (3):196–207.

Dinkmeyer, D. C. 1967. Elementary school guidance and the classroom teacher. *Elementary School Guidance and Counseling* 1 (1):15–26.

Dinkmeyer, D. C., and Caldwell, C. E. 1970. *Developmental counseling and guidance.* New York: McGraw-Hill.

Dinkmeyer, D. C., and Dreikurs, R. 1963. *Encouraging children to learn: The encouragement process.* Englewood Cliffs, N.J.: Prentice-Hall.

Dollard, J., and Miller, N. E. 1950. *Personality and psychotherapy.* New York: McGraw-Hill.

Dreikurs, R. 1968. *Psychology in one classroom.* New York: Harper & Row.

Dreyfus, E. A. 1967. Humanness: A therapeutic variable. *Personnel and Guidance Journal* 45 (6):573–577.

Ellis, A. 1962. *Reason and emotion in psychotherapy.* New York: Lyle Stuart.

Ford, D. H., and Urban, H. B. 1963. *Systems of psychotherapy.* New York: John Wiley and Sons.

Frankl, V. E. 1960. Paradoxical intention: A logotherapeutic technique. *American Journal of Psychotherapy* 14:520–535.

Frankl, V. E. 1962*a. Man's search for meaning.* Boston: Beacon Press.

Frankl, V. E. 1962*b.* Psychiatry and man's quest for meaning. *Journal of Religion and Health* 1:93–103.

Fullmer, D. W., and Bernard, H. W. 1972. *The school counselor-consultant.* New York: Houghton Mifflin Company.

Glasser, W. 1965. *Reality therapy.* New York: Harper & Row.

Glasser, W. 1969. *Schools without failure.* New York: Harper & Row.

Glasser, W. 1972. *The identity society.* New York: Harper & Row.

Glicken, M. D. 1968. Rational counseling: A dynamic approach to children. *Elementary School Guidance and Counseling* 2 (4):261–267.

Grubbe, T. E. 1968. Adlerian psychology as a basic framework for elementary school counseling services. *Elementary School Guidance and Counseling* 3 (1):20–26.

Hansen, J. C., Stevic, R. R., and Warner, R. W. 1972. *Counseling: Theory and process.* Boston: Allyn and Bacon.

Hillman, B. W. 1967. The parent-teacher education center: A supplement to elementary school counseling. *Elementary School Guidance and Counseling* 3 (2):111–117.

Hummel, R. C. 1962. Ego-counseling in guidance: Concept and method. *Harvard Educational Review* 32:463–482.

Kempler, W. 1973. Gestalt therapy. In Corsini, R., ed., Current psychotherapies. Itasca, Illinois: F. E. Peacock.

Krumboltz, J. D., and Thoresen, C. E. 1969. *Behavioral counseling.* New York: Holt, Rinehart and Winston.

Lister, J. L. 1967. Theory aversion in counselor education. *Counselor Education and Supervision* 6 (2):91–96.

Longstreth, L. E. 1968. *Psychological development of the child.* New York: Ronald Press.

May, R., Angel, E., and Ellenberger, H., eds. 1958. *Existence: A new dimension in psychiatry and psychology.* New York: Basic Books.

Patterson, C. H. 1965. Phenomenological psychology. *Personnel and Guidance* Journal 43 (10):997–1005.

Patterson, C. H. 1966, 2nd ed., 1973. *Theories of counseling and psychotherapy.* New York: Harper & Row.

Perls, F. S., Goodman, P., and Hefferline, R. F. 1951. *Gestalt therapy—Excitement and growth in human personality.* New York: Julian.

Perls, F. S., Hefferline, R., and Goodman, P. 1965. *Gestalt therapy.* New York: Dell.

Peters, H. J. 1963. Interference to guidance program development. *Personnel and Guidance Journal* 42:119–124.

Rogers, C. R. 1942. *Counseling and psychotherapy.* Boston: Houghton Mifflin.

Rogers, C. R. 1951. *Client-centered therapy.* Boston: Houghton Mifflin.

Rogers, C. R. 1961. *On becoming a person: A therapist's view of psychotherapy.* Boston: Houghton Mifflin.

Sahakian, W. S., ed. 1969. *Psychotherapy and counseling.* Chicago: Rand McNally.

Salter, A. 1961. *Conditioned reflex therapy: The direct approach to the reconstruction of personality.* New York: Capricorn.

Seeman, J. 1965. Client-centered therapy. In Wolman, B. B., ed., *Handbook of Clinical Psychology.* New York: McGraw-Hill.

Shertzer, B., and Stone, S. C. 1968, 2nd ed., 1974. *Fundamentals of counseling.* New York: Houghton Mifflin.

Skinner, B. F. 1953. *Science and human behavior* New York: Macmillan.

Sprinthall, N. A. 1971. *Guidance for human growth.* New York: Van Nostrand Reinhold Company.

Stefflre, B. 1965. Theories of counseling. New York: McGraw-Hill.

Thompson, E. A. 1967. Model for developmental counseling. *Elementary School Guidance and Counseling* 2 (2):135–142.

van Kaam, A. 1962. Counseling from the viewpoint of existential psychology. *Harvard Educational Review* 32 (4):403–415.

Williamson, E. G. 1950. *Counseling adolescents.* New York: McGraw-Hill.

Williamson, E. G. 1965. *Vocational counseling: Some historical, philosophical, and theoretical perspectives.* New York: McGraw-Hill.

Williamson, E. G. 1967. Youth's dilemma: To be or to become. *The Personnel and Guidance Journal* 46 (2):173–177.

Wolpe, J. 1958. *Psychotherapy by reciprocal inhibition.* Stanford: Stanford University Press.

Wolpe, J. 1969. *The practice of behavior therapy.* New York: Pergamon Press.

Glossary

ABILITY   A combination of skills, competence, and understanding based upon inherited capacities and experiences. The capacity to learn and perform.

ADAPTABLE   Having the ability to adjust to novel or prevailing circumstances.

AGGRESSION   Forceful action of an individual toward himself or others.

AMBIGUITY   Vagueness or uncertainty of meaning.

ANECDOTAL RECORD   A written report which describes unusual behavior of an individual.

ANXIETY   A state of arousal or tension or uneasiness of mind.

APPRAISAL   An assessment or estimate of value.

ASSOCIATION   A joining or connecting of two elements.

AUTOBIOGRAPHY   A self-written account of one's personal life.

AUTONOMY   A state of independent functioning.

BEHAVIOR   The conduct or reactions of an individual.

BEHAVIORAL   A form of counseling which stresses that behavior is learned.

BEHAVIORISM   Coined originally by J. B. Watson to indicate that habits may be explained in terms of glandular and motor reactions. Currently a theory of counseling (behavioral).

CAPACITY   The potential of an individual for learning or activity.

CHARACTER   Patterns of behavior or moral nature of an individual.

CLASSICAL CONDITIONING   A condition in which a neutral stimulus is paired with an unconditioned stimulus until the neutral one becomes a conditioned stimulus.

COMMITMENT   An agreement, pledge or decision of an individual to pursue a goal.

COMMONALITIES   Elements which characterize more than one theory or philosophy.

COMPETENCIES   Particular abilities or skills.

CONCEPT   An idea or belief generalized from existing information.

CONCEPTUAL   Kind of thought relating to a generalization of ideas.

CONDITIONING   To modify behavior so that an act previously associated with one stimulus becomes associated with another stimulus.

CONFIDENTIALITY   The assurance and responsibility to keep certain matters private and not divulge them.

CONGRUENT   A condition in which there is a close matching of awareness and experience.

CONSULTANT   An individual who gives professional advice and provides certain services.

CONSULTATION   The act of one individual conferring with another for the purpose of solving a problem.

COUNSELING   A service provided by a professionally trained individual to a person seeking help with personal problems.

COUNSELOR   A specialist in counseling; one who gives assistance with educational, vocational, or personal problems.

CREATIVITY   The ability to produce something novel and to think imaginatively.

CRITERIA   Standards by which judgments as to the quality of something may be determined.

CUMULATIVE RECORD   Record of basic educational data maintained on a student.

DEVELOPMENT   Changes in an organism which occur from birth to maturity.

DEVELOPMENTAL TASK   An achievement expected of a person at a particular stage of development which is critical to further achievement and happiness.

ECUMENICAL   Worldwide or general in extent, influence, or application.

EDUCATION   Process of teaching a child in a formal school setting.

EFFICACY   Effectiveness of a technique or procedure.

EGO   The problem solving portion of the personality.

ELECTRA COMPLEX   The female counterpart of the Oedipus complex: the erotic love a girl may have for her father.

EMPATHY   The ability to put oneself in the place of another person and to feel as that person does.

ENHANCEMENT   Increasing, making greater, or raising.

ENRICHMENT   Adding to the quality and breadth of an experience.

ENVIRONMENT   Everything external to the person with which he is in some relation.

EXISTENTIALISM   A kind of philosophy or point of view that has existence and its meaning as points of major emphasis.

EXPEDITER   A person who assumes responsibility for the functioning of a group.

EXPLOITATION   An unjust or improper use of another person for one's own profit or advantage.

EXPLORATION   Act of examining or investigating the possibilities of a resource.

FACILITATE   To make easier or to function more efficiently.

FIXATION   An obsession or unhealthy preoccupation or attachment with or to some inappropriate object or notion.

FLEXIBILITY   State of being capable of responding or conforming to changing or new situations.

FOSTER   To encourage or promote.

FREE ASSOCIATION Allowing the mind to wander and to deal with any idea or memory which comes freely to mind.

FULFILLMENT A condition of satisfaction or sense of achievement.

GROUP Several individuals assembled together for a common purpose.

GROUP COUNSELING The process of providing personal assistance to several individuals within a group setting.

GROUP DYNAMICS Interacting forces within a small group of individuals.

GROUP THERAPY Psychological services involving the application of therapeutic principles to a designated group of individuals seeking assistance in the resolution of psychological conflicts or difficulties.

GROWTH The process of progressive development and increase in complexity, size, or efficiency.

GROWTH COUNSELING A counseling approach that places considerable stress upon the development of the individual's internal resources as a source of strength and direction in resolving problems and capitalizing upon available growth opportunities.

GUIDANCE SERVICE One of the basic elements of educational service designed to assist students in planning and problem solving.

HYGIOLOGY A science or attitude which stresses the prevention of problems and maladjustment.

IMPLICATIONS The possible outcomes of a particular condition, or what should be done as a result of the condition.

INFORMATIONAL SERVICES That element of the guidance program which provides detailed information about the professions and vocations.

INHIBITIONS Inner feelings of impediments or restraints which deter a full expression of feeling.

INNOVATION Introduction of something new, such as a new method, idea, or device.

INSIGHT The gaining of an idea that makes sense, or the act of suddenly understanding a situation.

INTEGRAL   Being an essential part of something which adds to its completeness.

INTERACTION   A condition of mutual give and take of ideas or expressions.

INTERPERSONAL   A condition of personal interrelating between or among individuals.

INTUITION   The power of recognition or of assumed understanding without the benefit of direct knowledge.

INVOLVEMENT   The state of being closely associated with others in a meaningful activity.

KNOWLEDGE   Information obtained through experience.

LEARNING   An enduring change in behavior as a result of experience.

LIFESTYLE   A persistent pattern of thinking, feeling, and acting through which the individual seeks security and the feeling of superiority.

LIMITATION   A condition which restricts or restrains.

MALADJUSTMENT   Poor or inadequate adjustment based on behavior and personality characteristics.

MEDIA   Material and techniques used for bettering communication and growing insights.

MENTAL HEALTH   Patterns of behavior and qualities of personal adjustment.

MODEL   A person or thing that serves as a pattern to be emulated.

MORALITY   A condition of conformity to ideals or standards of human conduct and thought.

MOTIVATE   To stimulate another person toward appropriate action.

MOTIVATION   Forces that promote action toward the attainment of a goal.

MOTIVE   A condition which prompts action toward a goal.

MULTIPLE COUNSELING   A form of counseling which utilizes the group members in promoting better adjustment of all participants.

NEED   An internal condition that prompts action.

NEUROSIS   Deviant and undesirable personal characteristics and behavior.

NORMAL   Being near a norm or an average; free of abnormalities.

OBJECTIVE   Being an expression of reality as opposed to subjective judgments.

OEDIPUS COMPLEX   The sexual attraction a male child may have for his mother.

OPTIMUM   The greatest degree attained under implied or specified conditions.

PERSONALITY   The qualities and characteristics which a person possesses.

PLAY MEDIA   Materials and devices used in counseling and therapy to better communications and to facilitate adjustment.

PLAY THERAPY   A counseling or therapeutic technique by which better adjustment is attained.

POSITIVE REINFORCEMENT   Strengthening a response through the use of a positive reinforcer or reward.

POTENTIALITIES   Those inherent qualities or possibilities which are subject to development.

PREROGATIVE   An exclusive or special right, power, or privilege.

PRINCIPLE   A rule or guide based upon a philosophy or belief.

PRODUCTIVITY   The quality or state of being productive and of achieving goals.

PROFESSION   An organized vocational pursuit in which services are performed.

PSYCHOLOGIST   A specialist in the science of behavior.

PSYCHOSIS   Deviant behavior patterns and characteristics.

PSYCHOTHERAPY   A therapeutic service designed to bring about better behavior and adjustment patterns.

PUNITIVE   Characterized by punishing or getting even.

PUPIL INVENTORY   A record and accumulation of personal data utilized in guiding a child through school.

RAPPORT   The quality of the relationship between counselor and client, which involves feelings of warmth and mutual acceptance.

RATIONALIZATION   An explanation for behavior inconsistent with the facts.

REGRESSION   A return to an inappropriate pattern of behavior as a defense against problems.

REINFORCEMENT   The strengthening of a response.

RELATIONSHIP   A closeness involving interaction of one individual with another.

RESENTMENT   A feeling of displeasure toward someone whose behavior is disliked.

RESIGNATION   The act of giving up hope, of giving in to a condition.

ROLE   Behavior associated with a particular position in a group.

SELF-ACTUALIZATION   A condition of fulfillment in which an individual is realizing his potential.

SELF-ACTUALIZING   Characterized by the individual's meeting his needs and gaining satisfaction from his attainments.

SELF-CONCEPT   How one views and feels about himself.

SELF-CONFIDENCE   Belief in oneself and in one's powers and abilities.

SELF-DEPENDENCE   The degree to which one relies upon himself and his own resources.

SELF-ESTEEM   A pride in oneself, and the quality of one's self-regard.

SENSITIVITY TRAINING   A type of training which stresses experiencing with people and coming to know oneself better.

SOCIAL DEVELOPMENT   A form of development which concerns itself with skills of human relationships.

SOCIAL WORKER   A professionally trained person who works with individuals experiencing problems with possible societal causes.

SOCIO-PSYCHOLOGICAL   Associated with conditions related to society and one's psychological makeup.

STRUCTURE   An outline of principles or concepts which provides for making plans or conducting an activity.

SYMPTOM   A behavior that indicates the existence of an underlying cause.

SYNDROME   A group of symptoms which are indicative of an abnormality.

THEORY   An explanation of a condition or what might be expected to happen in a situation, such as in counseling.

THERAPY   A professional service by which the individual may bring about new insights and improved behavior.

TRADITIONAL   A long-term and well-established way of thinking or doing something.

TRAUMA   A disordered psychic or behavioral state resulting from mental or emotional stress or physical injury.

UNDERACHIEVEMENT   A condition marking a performance below what might be expected in view of the individual's capacities.

VALUES   Goals or beliefs of some depth and permanence to which an individual has a strong commitment.

Index

About the Author

Lester N. Downing is a professor of educational psychology, specializing in counseling psychology, at Brigham Young University. He holds the Ed.D. degree in Educational Psychology, and is a member of the American Personnel and Guidance Association, the Association for Counselor Education and Supervision, and the International Transactional Analysis Association. He is the author of *120 Readings in Guidance, Guidance and Counseling Services,* and *Guidance and Counseling in Current Education.* And he has written numerous articles on education and counseling which have appeared in national journals.